# The Rhythm of Eternity

# Dissident Biographies

Edited by Rohan B. E. Price

## Vol 1

James King

# The Rhythm of Eternity

The Life and Art of Rockwell Kent

**PETER LANG**

New York · Berlin · Bruxelles · Chennai · Lausanne · Oxford

Bibliographic information published by the Deutsche Nationalbibliothek
The German National Library lists this publication in the German National Bibliography;
detailed bibliographic data is available on the Internet at http://dnb.d-nb.de.

Library of Congress Cataloging-in-Publication Data
Names: King, James, 1942- author
Title: The Rhythm of Eternity : The life and Art of Rockwell Kent / James King.
Description: New York : Peter Lang, [2026] | Series: Dissident biographies | Includes bibliographical references and index.
Identifiers: LCCN 2026003291 (print) | LCCN 2026003292 (ebook) | ISBN 9783034356343 paperback | ISBN 9783034356350 ebook | ISBN 9783034356367 epub
Subjects: LCSH: Kent, Rockwell, 1882-1971--Psychology | Artists--United States--Biography | LCGFT: Biographies
Classification: LCC N6537.K44 K56 2026 (print) | LCC N6537.K44 (ebook)
LC record available at https://lccn.loc.gov/2026003291
LC ebook record available at https://lccn.loc.gov/2026003292

Cover Image: Rockwell Kent. *Self-portrait. Voyaging.* 1924.

ISSN 3070-0132
ISBN 978-3-0343-5634-3 (Print)
ISBN 978-3-0343-5635-0 (ePDF)
ISBN 978-3-0343-5636-7 (ePUB)
DOI 10.3726/b23479

© 2026 Peter Lang Group AG, Lausanne, Switzerland
Published by Peter Lang Publishing Inc., New York, USA

info@peterlang.com

All rights reserved.
All parts of this publication are protected by copyright.
Any utilization outside the strict limits of the copyright law, without the permission of the publisher, is forbidden and liable to prosecution. This applies in particular to reproductions, translations, microfilming, and storage and processing in electronic retrieval systems.

This publication has been peer reviewed.

Contact for General Product Safety Regulation (GPSR): gpsr@peterlang.com

www.peterlang.com

# Contents

List of Figures … vii
Preface … ix
Acknowledgments … xi

Introduction: The Contrarian … 1

CHAPTER 1
The Lost Boy (1882–1887) … 7

CHAPTER 2
Apprentice (1888–1905) … 11

CHAPTER 3
Laborer (1905–1907) … 17

CHAPTER 4
The "Self" and the "Better Self" (1908–1911) … 23

CHAPTER 5
Carpenter (1910–1913) … 29

CHAPTER 6
Expatriate (1914–1915) … 35

CHAPTER 7
Satirist (1915–1918) … 43

CONTENTS

CHAPTER 8
Survivor (1918–1919) ........................................................ 51

CHAPTER 9
Gentleman Farmer (1919–1922) .................................... 69

CHAPTER 10
Lover (1922–1928) ............................................................. 75

CHAPTER 11
Illustrator (1925–1949) ..................................................... 85

CHAPTER 12
Explorer (1929–1932) ........................................................ 93

CHAPTER 13
Advocate (1933–1945) ...................................................... 97

CHAPTER 14
Politico (1945–1971) .......................................................... 103

Epilogue by Way of Four Self-Portraits ......................... 111

Short Titles and Abbreviations ....................................... 121

Endnotes ............................................................................. 123

Index .................................................................................... 129

# Figures

Figure 1: Rockwell Kent in Punta Arenas, Chile. 1922. Photographer unknown ... 1
Figure 2: *Toilers of the Sea*. 1907. 96.5 × 118 cm. Oil on canvas. New Britain Museum of Art ... 20
Figure 3: *Winter, Monhegan Island*. 1907. Oil on canvas. 86 × 118 cm. Metropolitans Museum of Art ... 21
Figure 4: *Men and Mountains*. 1909. Oil on canvas. 83.8 × 109.8 cm. Columbus Museum of Art ... 27
Figure 5: *Down to the Sea*. 1910. Oil on canvas. 108 × 142.9 cm. Brooklyn Museum ... 37
Figure 6: *Burial of a Young Man*. c. 1908–1911. Oil on canvas. 71 × 133 cm. Phillips Collection ... 38
Figure 7: *The House of Dread*. c. 1914–1917. Oil on canvas. 70.5 × 95.9 cm. Plattsburgh State Art Museum ... 39
Figure 8: *Portrait of a Child (My Daughter Clara)*. 1914. Oil on canvas. 54 × 72 cm. Pushkin State Museum of Fine Arts ... 41
Figure 9: Drawings by "Hogarth, Jr." for *Vanity Fair, Puck* and *A Basket of Poses*. 1915–1924 ... 45
Figure 10: *Alaska Winter*. 1919. Oil on canvas. 86 × 110 cm. Anchorage Museum ... 54
Figure 11: *Resurrection Bay, Alaska (Blue and Gold)*. 1919. 30 × 38 cm. Bowdoin College ... 54

FIGURES

| | | |
|---|---|---|
| Figure 12: | *North Wind.* 1919. Oil on canvas mounted on hardboard. 104 × 86 cm. The Phillips Collection | 55 |
| Figure 13: | Frontispiece. *Wilderness.* 1920. Private Collection | 57 |
| Figure 14: | Dedication Page. *Wilderness.* 1920. Private Collection | 59 |
| Figure 15: | Home Building. *Wilderness.* 1920. Private Collection | 61 |
| Figure 16: | On the Height. *Wilderness.* 1920. Private Collection | 63 |
| Figure 17: | The Mad Hermit. *Wilderness.* 1920. Private Collection | 65 |
| Figure 18: | *The Trapper.* 1921. Oil on canvas. 86 × 112 cm. Whitney Museum of American Art | 73 |
| Figure 19: | *Admiralty Sound, Tierra del Fuego.* 1925. 86 × 111 cm. Oil on canvas. Heritage Museum, Saint Petersburg | 79 |
| Figure 20: | Ahab. *Moby Dick.* 1930 | 88 |
| Figure 21: | Moby Dick. *Moby Dick.* 1930 | 89 |
| Figure 22: | Frontispiece. *Leaves of Grass.* 1936 | 90 |
| Figure 23: | Illustrations from *Paul Bunyan.* 1941 | 91 |
| Figure 24: | *Early November, North Greenland.* 1932. Oil on canvas. 86 × 110 cm. Hermitage Museum, Saint Petersburg | 96 |
| Figure 25: | *December Eight, 1941 (The Open Road).* 1941. Oil on canvas. 109 × 180 cm. Plattsburgh State Art Museum | 102 |
| Figure 26: | *Heavy, Heavy Hangs over Thy Head.* 1946. Lithograph. 23 × 30 cm. Metropolitan Museum of Art | 104 |
| Figure 27: | *Golden Autumn.* c. 1955. Oil on canvas. 71 × 86 cm. Private Collection | 109 |
| Figure 28: | *Portrait of Me Improved.* Frontispiece to *Voyaging.* 1924. Private Collection | 111 |
| Figure 29: | *Sea and Sky.* Wood engraving. 1931–1932. 25.4 × 17 cm. Private Collection | 113 |
| Figure 30: | *Self-Portrait.* Lithograph on stone. 1934. 35 × 25.4 cm. Private Collection | 115 |
| Figure 31: | Self-portrait. *Voyaging.* 1924. Color woodcut. 15 × 15 cm. Private Collection | 117 |

# Preface

Biographies come in many guises. Some glance at every corner of a subject's life in such fine detail that minutiae often overpower the resulting narrative and are so clogged with facts that the subject gets lost. Others examine a person's existence from a fixed point of view so that the only evidence provided supports that thesis.

Short biographies are strange creatures with their own rules. By definition, they look at and examine an individual's life with, as Lytton Strachey put it, "a brevity which excludes everything that is redundant and nothing that is significant." This is not an easy task, although it is a worthwhile one if the character and accomplishments of the subject are brought into focus.

This brief narrative focuses on Rockwell Kent, the artist. My aim has been to delineate the force of his extraordinary personality while also evaluating his accomplishments. He was a person whose life was strewn with paradoxes and inconsistencies. Kent, a man of charm and vitality, led an outwardly tempestuous existence—especially in affairs of the heart—but, at the very same time, he created much of his best art in solitude. He was an incredible romantic who fell violently in love and then decisively out of it. He loved many women, but he thought only of his own needs in his relationships with them—in this regard, he thought the profession of artist gave him leeway to think only of his own needs. He strove, sometimes with great difficulty, to achieve material needs, but his art is replete with transcendental yearnings. He craved many of the comforts of bourgeois existence, but he remained a dedicated socialist even when his politics led to a diminishment of interest in his art. He sometimes lived an apparently blithe existence, but he experienced great inner torment.

## PREFACE

In 1955, at the age of 73, Kent published an autobiography: *It's Me O Lord*. In that often-rambling narrative, his personality and character can be vividly heard—as a storyteller he possessed a strong, compelling voice. However, he was an unreliable narrator, one who requires frequent fact-checking. As an older man, he often misremembered or fabricated events in his early life. In constructing my narrative, I allow Kent to speak, but I also point out where he is leading the reader astray. Using this approach, I have tried to provide a portrait of this paradoxical man.

Kent was a man of many guises, and in writing his life I have told his story chronologically. However, in each of the chapters, I have focused on one of those roles, although they often overlap. One truth stands out. Despite the many inconsistencies in his character, Kent was single-minded in his career as an artist. He wanted to capture the "rhythm of eternity."[1] In his paintings, drawings, prints, and illustrated books, there is a purity of purpose and completeness of execution that make him a great artist.

# Acknowledgments

David Traxel's biography of Kent (1980) provides a detailed, chronological account of his life. Since its publication, many new pieces of information about Kent have come to light, and I have incorporated them into my narrative. Traxel provides little critical analysis of Kent's art, and my account is focused on examining the relationship between Kent's life and his artistic production.

Scholars and writers such as Dan Burne-Jones, Doug Capra, Scott R. Ferris, Jamie Franklin, Fridolf Johnson, Constance Martin, Ellen Pearce, Caroline Welsh, and Richard V. West have made important contributions to our understanding of Kent. In researching this brief account of Kent's life, I remain deeply indebted to the magisterial scholarship of Jake Milgram Wien.

# Introduction: The Contrarian

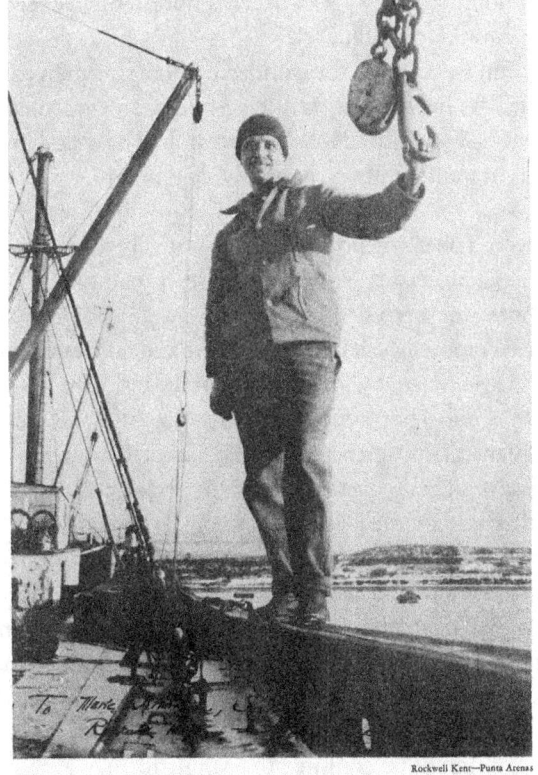

**Figure 1:** Rockwell Kent in Punta Arenas, Chile. 1922. Photographer unknown.

INTRODUCTION: THE CONTRARIAN

In 1932, at the age of 40, Rockwell Kent—artist, writer and adventurer—had become a celebrity. That year, Alfred A. Knopf published a small book about him by the designer, producer and cultural critic Merle Armitage, who observed: "Kent's position—his success in so many fields and his nation-wide popularity—is so much taken for granted that he has become an accepted part of our American scene. That in his almost unprecedented career he has hurdled obstacles of the most formidable character is certainly not common knowledge. He is one of the most interesting phenomena of our times."[2]

Facing the title page is a photograph of a smiling, athletic-looking, middle-aged man in fisherman's garb staring into the distance. He makes no eye contact with the viewer. Kent the visionary can be glimpsed here, but the snapshot does not match any pre-conceived notion the reader might have of what an artist should look like.

The reader can be forgiven for wondering how this man can be a serious artist. How had he become, as Armitage put it, an "accepted part of [the] American scene"? What formidable "obstacles" had he overcome? What facets of his life had catapulted him to nation-wide renown?

Kent was, indeed, a phenomenon. At a comparatively young age, he had established himself as a successful artist. The landscape paintings—products of his travels to remote and often desolate regions—were exhibited and for sale at well-established commercial galleries. He wrote and illustrated books about his adventures and also illustrated the works of writers as diverse as Shakespeare, Voltaire, Melville and Thornton Wilder. His drawings and wood engravings garnered popular acclaim and brisk sales. He accepted numerous commissions for bookplates, designed advertisements for major corporations, and even invented an alternate artistic personality under the pseudonym "Hogarth, Jr."

Everyone who encountered Kent was struck by his charisma. Yet one unidentified friend lamented that he had squandered his gifts; according to this person, he had overextended himself in the realm of commercial art to the detriment of his deeper talents. This diffusion—doing so many different things—was seen as a threat to his artistic standing. What this criticism overlooked was Kent's essential nature as a polymath: an artist of vast range whose talents could not be confined to a single form.

Armitage echoed this anonymous critique, ending his book with a prediction that in time "Kent's misdeeds of commercial art, his rebellion against reactionary influences, his flamboyant living, and his romantic adventuring will have been forgiven and forgotten."³ Kent's enduring artistic achievements, he believed, would ultimately eclipse any perceived flaws.

Kent could be impulsive, generous, and idealistic—but also calculating, narrow-minded, insensitive, and petty. His profuse talents were never entirely under his control. He was stubborn, questioned authority and dismissed orthodoxy. In this sense, he was a contrarian—an original spirit whose rejection of convention made him both admired and misunderstood.

As an artist, Kent challenged the incredible stranglehold that the School of Paris held over American art. That vicelike grip, Armitage observed, spoke "with the still, small, penetrating voice of finality ... In a silence more eloquent than protestation, [its] superiority is taken for granted ... Long before realizing what has happened, you are yourself part of... this vast machine."⁴

Although other American artists—his teachers and peers—had asserted that American modernism should never subserviently copycat European modernism—Kent became a leading voice in the call for independence. For him, an American artist—damn the consequences—had to pursue his own distinct path.

Kent was a dissenter in many other ways. Like some intellectuals of his generation, he found inspiration and solace in the transcendentalist writings of Ralph Waldo Emerson and Henry David Thoreau. He embraced their belief in the spiritual essence of nature and human experience. For Kent, art had to express not just surface appearance but inner truth—the symbolic kernel beneath the visible shell.

In this way, Kent's transcendentalism, like Walt Whitman's, fused spiritual values with social ones. Despite his privileged background, Kent, from a young age, identified with members of the working class. This affinity formed the bedrock of his lifelong commitment to socialism and his break with bourgeois values. He believed that an American artist had a moral obligation to stand in solidarity with all citizens.

And yet, paradoxically, Kent was no stranger to elite society. Under the name "Hogarth, Jr." he published humorous drawings in *Vanity Fair* and other magazines lampooning the foibles of the Manhattan café society he himself often frequented.

## INTRODUCTION: THE CONTRARIAN

As a young man, Kent conceived of masculinity in conventional, late Victorian terms. Women were exalted; marriage channeled a man's sexuality. In adulthood, he turned against what he ironically called his "Better Self," that side of his character that had espoused—and practiced—conventional, societal values.

Kent also drew a distinction between those who merely endure life and those who embrace it. "There are two kinds of people," he wrote. "There are those who cannot bear happiness ... They live vicariously. But there are others to whom life is so beautiful that their whole experience of it keeps them in a constant turmoil of excitement and enthusiasm."[5] Kent considered himself one of the latter.

He also saw himself as someone who had defied, not succumbed to, his instincts. "The most profound incentive of my whole life," he wrote, "has been overcoming that lazy, slothful, sensuous being that I maybe am. I suspect that I get up in the morning because I want to lie in bed; that I exercise because I want to sleep; that I work because I am essentially lazy; that I want to accomplish something because I have a profound contempt for accomplishment."[6] He worked, he claimed, because he was essentially slothful. For Kent, living fully meant battling inertia.

This fervent embrace of life extended into his relationships, often to the detriment of those around him. He expected those close to him to share his passions, regardless of their own needs or objections. At times, he envisioned himself as a kind of Nietzschean superman—an irresistible force bending others to his will. Yet beneath this imposing public persona lay a private man prone to despondency.

Although born in Tarrytown, New York, and residing at times in New York City, Vermont, and upstate New York, Kent's imagination was stirred most profoundly by remote, unfamiliar places: Maine, Newfoundland, Alaska, Tierra del Fuego, Ireland, and Greenland. These locales, far removed from urban routine, offered him creative refuge and spiritual renewal. They also became stages on which he explored his inner landscape through words and images.

In his sweeping autobiography, *It's Me O Lord* (1955), Kent recounted his journey as an artist with candor. He described the hardships—financial and emotional—he had faced. A masterful storyteller, he knew how to charm,

INTRODUCTION: THE CONTRARIAN

confide, and withhold. He presented himself as both humble and grandiose and cast himself, quite consciously, as the hero of his own narrative—a modern-day David Copperfield. Yet Kent's unspoken autobiography resides in his art. In his landscapes, a mystical presence hovers beneath the visible world. In his wood engravings and drawings, he created a symbolic mythology of the self—one that oscillated between exultation and despair.

In telling the story of Kent's life and art, I have sought to bring into focus the dynamic interplay between his public persona and his private self. But Kent's legacy must be judged by his accomplishments. What did he achieve as an artist and writer? How did politics shape his art? Who was this man who challenged the conventions of his time with such passionate conviction? Why does he still matter? This account attempts to answer those questions.

CHAPTER 1

# The Lost Boy (1882–1887)

"Babies, like acorns, fall from trees, from family trees; and if we are interested in what the little seed may come to be, we have but to look upon the tree whence it fell."[7] Guided by this observation, Kent began his autobiography with an account of his ancestors' arrival in North America. His father's family prospered to the extent that the artist's father, George Rockwell Kent (1853–1887) was educated at Phillips Exeter, Yale and Harvard before attending law school at Columbia and then setting up practice in New York City.

Sara Ann Holgate Kent (1854–1947) Kent Senior's future wife, had a far less stable upbringing. Her father's business ventures took the family from one factory town to another. At the age of 11, Sara was sent to live with her mother's extremely wealthy sister and brother-in-law, Josie and James Banker, at their estate in Irvington, New York. The Bankers' only child had died, and Sara became their surrogate daughter.

As a youngster, although surrounded by riches, Sara was both unhappy and rebellious. Although James Banker revered her, he sought to curb the child's unruly nature. When she turned 20 and of marriageable age, Banker insisted no one was good enough for her. He did not wish her to leave home, and he prevented her leaving the house if he suspected she was meeting a suitor. Banker's plans went afoul when Sara met and fell in love with Kent. The two met clandestinely despite the precautions taken by Banker, who angrily rejected Kent's request for Sara's hand. The couple had no choice but to elope. Sara was disinherited.

CHAPTER 1

Although the conflict between Sara and her uncle overshadowed her early married life, the Kents were prosperous. Rockwell became a full partner in a prestigious law firm and traveled widely in pursuit of money-making mining ventures. The couple lived in Tarrytown, New York in the spring and fall; they moved to New York City for the winter and spent their summers at a cottage at Shinnecock in Baytown, Long Island.

It was at Tarrytown, a village in the town of Greenburgh in Westchester County approximately 25 miles north of midtown Manhattan, that Rockwell Kent II was born on June 21, 1882 (his brother Douglas two years later). The young family's lifestyle was comfortable. Rosa, an Austrian-born maid, looked after the children. As a child, Rockwell was so close to her that he spoke German before English. Husband and wife shared an interest in art. Away from the office, Rockwell Senior played the flute and did woodwork.

That tranquil, affluent existence came to a halt in September 1887 when upon his return from a business trip to Guatemala, Rockwell Senior was struck down by typhoid fever. The young widow, pregnant with her third child, was left in severely depleted financial circumstances. The townhouse in New York City was given up, and the small family took a "gloomy little row house"[8] house in Tarrytown. Sara's mother moved in with her to assist in raising the children. When James Banker died, his widow occasionally allowed the family to live with her at her estate when Sara was able to find someone to rent her new home.

Rockwell had been born to an affluence that suddenly vanished. His childhood memories were composed of a mixture of luxury and deprivation. He was never quite sure where he fitted in. By all accounts, this small, wiry boy became difficult and obstinate. What he possessed in abundance was his mother's rebellious streak. Sara could not discipline a child who refused to bend to her will. Emotionally, he was her son.

Since Sara, a reserved, contained individual, never spoke of her late husband, Rockwell retained only fragmentary memories of him. It was as if an essential part of his existence had been cut away. He did not want his memory of his father to be erased: he treasured his father's flute and carried it with him on his travels. But who was this man who had vanished? What was the connection between father and son? This issue haunted him.

## THE LOST BOY (1882–1887)

Many years later, Kent asked a chirographer to analyze his father's handwriting. The result revealed that Rockwell Senior demonstrated in his personality "all the assets—but equally all the shortcomings—of a warm and rich heart." He also possessed "emotional impressibility."

> He was openly and ingenuously warm-hearted and, lacking diplomacy, was frank and truthful in his dealing with others, being utterly free of dissimulation and pretence. Though highly emotional ... he possessed an inner balance or harmony that was basic to his feeling that the world was ONE. He loved not only man but all of nature, life itself.[9]

The analysis confirmed what Kent "had heard from those who had known my father, and nowhere contradicts them."[10] In this instance, the artist responded so positively because he saw what he wanted to see: he and his father shared many personality traits. In later life, Kent felt a keen sense of loss for the father who had been precipitously snatched away from him. He revisited that wound in his art and writings.

# Apprentice (1888–1905)

The loss of her husband inhibited Sara, who became a demanding, overly protective parent. One of her strictly enforced rules was that Rockwell and his brother were forbidden to play with the neighborhood boys whom she perceived as from the lower class; for her, Rockwell remembered, "working people—those whose lot it was to do the hardest or more menial work—were of a different and lower order of mankind."[11]

The child's first school was, unfortunately, Miss Bennett's School for Girls, where too anxious to ask where the toilet was, he frequently wet his pants; from there he became a day student at an establishment in Tarrytown.

Impatient and often disappointed, Sara may have overreacted to her older son's fiery temperament when she sent him, at the age of the ten, to a local boarding school and, a year later, to the military-style Episcopal Academy at Cheshire, Connecticut, where he remained until 1896. Although an adequate student, he saw no reason to study Latin and would not bend to the will of its teacher. For him, his stay there was "tantamount to a seasonal orphanage. The qualities for "survival" under these educational circumstances were of a belligerent rather than an endearing nature."[12]

While Rockwell was at Cheshire, Sara's sister, Josephine (Jo) moved in with the family. Her temperament was very much like her sibling's and when Rockwell rebelled, she would thrash him with a gold-handled horsewhip. The last time she attempted to beat him, the boy grabbed the whip and buried it under an oak tree.[13]

Aunt and nephew were sufficiently reconciled that, at the age of 13, he traveled to England, the Netherlands and Germany with her. A year later,

## CHAPTER 2

Kent was allowed to return home from boarding school and become a day student at the Horace Mann School in New York City on 124$^{th}$ Street behind the Columbia University gymnasium. There, "manual training" was an essential part of the curriculum: "It enlarged the horizons of my life, opening channels of activity that were subsequently to lead me, on one hand into the ranks of labor and, on the other, to that *respect* for craftsmanship, which … I hold to be fundamental to the practice of all art."[14]

A year later, at the age of 15, Kent "began to practice art as a professional."[15] That was not a vocation of which his mother approved. Perhaps realizing her son's aptitude for "manual training" might be best extended to the study of a hands-on profession like architecture, she decided that the eighteen-year-old would study it at Columbia. For Kent, the course was initially a godsend. He became particularly adept at architectural drafting.

However, an obstacle for a successful career in that profession soon presented itself. Before Kent began at Columbia in the autumn of 1900, Sara Kent decided that the family would spend the summer in the cottage at Shinnecock that had been rented out since the death of her husband. Kent enrolled at William Merritt Chase's Shinnecock Hills Summer School. That decision transformed the feckless young man's future.

Although he had studied at that school as a youngster, that summer was different: "No student at Shinnecock can ever have devoted himself to his work with greater energy. All of every morning and of every afternoon I would be out of doors, my easel set up … All day I'd paint."[16] His commitment to landscape painting was born.

Kent was gratified by the cautious praise Chase lavished on him. In his second year at the school (1901), he was awarded a class prize; the following summer (1902), he won a prize to study at the New York School of Art (formerly called the Chase School of Art).

He developed a grudging respect for Chase and relished his encouragement. Things quickly changed. The more time Kent spent with Chase, the more he became disillusioned. For the young would-be artist, Chase was more interested in *"impressions"* of the subject than in deeper and more labored probing." If at one time he had been a respected father figure, "the Master" became a huge disappointment. He was a "little man, dapper in dress to the point of foppishness" who told his students: "Look at me … Beginning as a shoe clerk … I have come to be to the guest of kings."[17] For Chase, art was a commodity—a product for sale. For the disabused protégé, Chase's great crime was that he told students to paint what they saw without allowing room for self-expression. From 1900 to 1903, Kent tried to balance his commitment to architecture with his growing conviction that his destiny was to become an artist. In November 1900, when he was a freshman at Columbia, he took an evening lecture course with Arthur Wesley Dow at the Art Students League; in spring 1903, a night class with Robert Henri; he worked as an assistant to Abbott Handerson Thayer in the summer of 1903. That autumn, he quit Columbia and enrolled at the New York School of Art, where, he studied with Henri and Kenneth Hayes Miller until spring 1905.

American art was in crisis mode at the time Kent decided to become an artist. Most leading artists had studied in Europe and emulated trends in England and on the continent. There was not yet a distinctly American brand of modernist art. Robert Henri was among the first to forge one. A rebel like Kent, he was also drawn to the Transcendentalists—Ralph Waldo Emerson, Henry Thoreau and Margaret Fuller—who had created a distinctly American form of literature that maintained that each individual contained godlike potential, that the self must monitor its inner core, that a close relationship with nature was essential, and that a divine presence hovered on the periphery of material existence. In poetry, Walt Whitman had explored the implications of that philosophy by capturing the vitality he saw in daily life—its turmoil and disorder—and by emphasizing the spiritual values underscoring it. In American art, no such movement yet existed.

Henri sought to capture the turbulence in American life and helped found the so-called Ashcan School, whose members included George Bellows and his depictions of action-packed boxing matches and John Sloan's inner-city tenement views. Kent admired Henri's "interest in labor, underprivilege and dilapidation as the subject or background for a picture" that revealed "his own humanity." Henri valued felt experience over technical polish.

*Quality* he sought: the weight, the warmth, the loveliness of flesh, the grace of movement, gesture, the whole imponderable dignity of man. Less what our eyes could see than what was *felt*: and if the expression of such feeling appeared, in what we did, as undisciplined and sometimes chaotic as feelings essentially are; if knowledge was discounted and craftsmanship contemned, these were but casualties in a greater cause, their loss the means towards a noble end.[18]

CHAPTER 2

Chase had taught his student to use their eyes; Henri taught them to enlist their hearts. Like Whitman, Henri embraced life in America in its enormous vitality.

Henri's teaching style was unorthodox. One student recalled, "Sometimes he would just dribble along and then, suddenly, [he] would hit upon an idea and golden moments would follow." He sometimes ordered his charges: "Work with great speed ... Have your energies alert, up and active." He also instructed them: "Be a man first, be an artist later."[19] Kent took that advice to heart. Unlike Henri and the other Ashcan artists, Kent was not drawn to urban life or portraiture. He committed himself to landscapes infused with his own subjectivity.

From 1903 to 1905, Kent worked at various times as an assistant to the eccentric painter and naturalist Abbott Handerson Thayer in Dublin, New Hampshire. Kent's relationship with the older artist was more personal than professional: "in the qualities of his mind he was akin to the men of Concord, Emerson and Thoreau, whom he revered." Kent especially admired how Thayer "was all but fanatically exacting of himself and others in respect to truth in every detail of a statement, to truth as embodied in each word ... He was precious in his demand for exactitude of expression."[20] Thayer also introduced his assistant in Nordic mythology and German literature and music.

Kent's time in New York City brought him into touch with the plight of the working class, especially those that had immigrated to the United States. As a child he had witnessed his family's fall into financial insecurity and knew firsthand what it was to be a poor relation. Henri's influence had deepened his awareness of social injustice.

Earlier, as a youngster, he had been indoctrinated in socialism when he attended the "sociables" meetings convened by Rufus Weeks, the philanthropist, at the Community House and Library in Pocantico Hills, a hamlet near Tarrytown. The millionaire was a socialist with whom Kent could discuss "the origin and existence of privilege and its transmission to unworthy heirs; the concentration of great wealth in hands that had not labored to create it; the existence of poverty in a land of plenty." Weeks insisted: "No man may be termed 'intelligent' who is not a revolutionist."[21] These stirring words moved Kent. In 1904, he attended his first socialist meeting with Weeks. In 1908, the artist joined the socialist party.

Kent rebelliousness now had a political focus. Rejecting what he saw as the timid modernism of conservative American art, he embraced Henri's example and became, for the rest of his life, a staunch advocate of socialist principles—an inclination perhaps reinforced by his mother's disdain for the working class.

CHAPTER 3

# Laborer (1905–1907)

In the spring of 1904, Kent exhibited with the Society of American Artists and sold two paintings. To support himself while attempting to establish himself in his calling, he worked in Manhattan as a draftsman for a new architectural firm, Ewing and Chappell. George Chappell was a close friend; Charles Ewing had purchased one of the two paintings sold at the Society of American Artists. For the next ten years Kent worked for them intermittently.

At this time, Kent penned a vivid, unflattering, self-portrait:

> He isn't tall, being no more than five feet nine. He isn't broad-shouldered, he is altogether on the slender side, weighing only about one hundred and forty-five pounds ... he is fair-haired ... His eyes are brown, his brow is lofty (a euphemism, of course, for approaching baldness). His mouth is generous ... But his chin, on the other hand, is decidedly stingy, giving his profile the look, as his mother described it, of a duck about to quack.[22]

As Kent was aware, there were also flaws in his character. He was easily bored; he was also restless. When Robert Henri recommended an ideal spot for landscape painting—the artists' colony on the island of Monhegan, 12 nautical miles from the coast of Maine—Kent traveled there in the summer of 1905. He was immediately captivated by the majestic beauty of the island and the rugged lifestyle of the year-round residents.

> its rock-bound shores, its towering headlands, the thundering surf, with gleaming crests and emerald eddies, its forest and its flowering meadowlands; the village, quaint and picturesque; the fish-houses, evoking in their dilapidation those sad thoughts on the passage of time, and the transitoriness of all things human so dear to the artistic soul; and the *people*, those hardy fisherfolk, those men garbed in their sea boots and their black or yellow oil skins, those horny-handed sons of toil.[23]

## CHAPTER 3

He wrote Henri: "This place is more wonderful & beautiful than you told me it was. I've been here almost three weeks and haven't got over my amazement yet. It seems to me now that I'd like to paint here always."[24]

That fall, Kent reluctantly returned to the daily grind of his work in Manhattan, where he had settled to bide his time in establishing himself in the art world. That plan no longer seemed feasible. In 1906, he abandoned that scheme and moved to Monhegan.

The rugged terrain of Monhegan may have been the perfect setting for Kent's art, but he had to earn a living. In Manhattan, he had become attuned to the daily struggles facing the working poor. On Monhegan, his nascent socialist views encouraged him to put theory into practice. He reflected: "for the first time I saw my work in perspective." He envied these toilers of the sea and came into contact "with those social and political convictions, which had hitherto existed as figments of my heart and mind." He asked himself: "What would I do, I thought, should working men not work for me? The answer shamed me."[25] He envied those men "their strength ... their knowledge of boats and their familiarity with that awesome portion of the infinite, the sea. I envied them their worker's human dignity."[26] Determined to overcome what he saw as an inferiority complex, he took up manual labor: "there was something I could do about it: get to work."[27] On Monhegan, Kent became an artist-laborer. In doing so, he aligned himself with the trend of men seeking to restore a sense of physical vigor and masculinity through outdoor living.

In Henry James's *The Bostonians* (1885), the conservative-minded Basil Ransome confronts a situation challenging men at the turn of the century: "The whole generation is womanized: it's a feminine, nervous, hysterical, chattering, canting age ... The masculine character, the ability to dare and endure, to know and yet not fear reality, to look the world in the face and take it for what it is ... that is what I want to preserve, or rather ...recover."[28]

One way for men to "recover" was to live outdoors. During his stays with Thayer in Dublin, Kent had witnessed and participated in his mentor's devotion to outdoor living: "In the main house the windows were kept open all winter, and we sat at meals, heavily clothed, with a blazing fire on one side, and the breath of the arctic on the other ... the entire family slept out of doors, in all weathers and seasons, sheltered beneath open-sided shacks."[29]

## LABORER (1905-1907)

As the sociologist Michael Kimmel has observed: "the turn of the century reinvented the frontier as simply the outdoors." Theodore Roosevelt was among the "effete eastern intellectuals who spent time on ... civilized western ranches and rediscovered their manhood."[30]

In Maine, Kent put socialist theories into practice by transforming himself into a working man. He also discovered a way to assert his masculinity by living in a rugged, challenging environment. In 1906, he built a house for himself on Horn's Hill; two years later, Sara Kent—restored to financial security by a legacy from her deceased Aunt Josie—commissioned her son to build a house for her at Lobster Cove.

Kent kept in touch with the art world in New York City and periodically returned there. His first one-man show was at Clausen Galleries in 1907. The exhibition, devoted to 12 Monhegan landscapes, established Kent as an emerging talent. Henri declared that the canvases proved the young artist was "absorbed [into] the civilization in which he was living."[31] In *The Sun*, James Huneker claimed: "The paint is laid on by an athlete of the brush. Dissonances are dared that make you pull up your coat collar."[32] The artist Guy Pène Du Bois celebrated the canvases as American in a new, distinctly modern way:

> In method, idea, suggestion and composition [these paintings] are absolutely American; there is not one inch of anything else in them. They have precision, economy, dignity and force. They breathe the free open air and the poetry in the clearness of it ... Kent gets marvelously the solidity of the rocks, the depth and heaviness of water and the positive strength of our Maine fisherman.[33]

Despite the acclaim, nothing sold.

This series of landscapes brought together strands with which Kent had been toying. He allowed his emotional contact with the island to come to the fore in forceful brush strokes, in vivid contrasts between land and water, and in the juxtaposition of strong colors in close proximity to each other. Elemental features frequently jostle with each other.

In *Toilers of the Sea* (1907), fishermen battle with strong waves beneath a majestic cliff. The sea's abstract swirls of blue and white merge with the rock. Like Whitman, Kent celebrated the perilous day-to-struggles of laborers. In this seafaring image, Kent was following in the tradition of Winslow Homer, but Kent emphasized the swelling sea in contrast to Homer's usual attention to human protagonists.[34]

CHAPTER 3

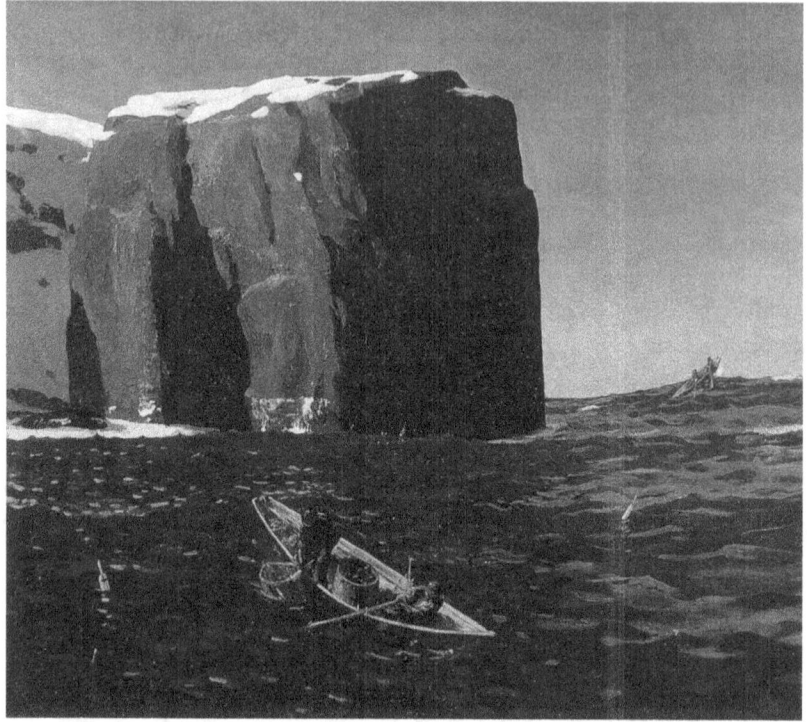

**Figure 2:** *Toilers of the Sea*. 1907. 96.5 × 118 cm. Oil on canvas. New Britain Museum of Art.

Two of Kent's fellow students at the New York School of Art were so taken with the Monhegan canvases that they journeyed there to paint: George Bellows in 1911, Edward Hopper in 1916. Bellows was aroused by the "dark mysteries" that Kent had captured on Monhegan. Critics noted parallels between Hopper and Kent in how they handled "the dramatic effects of light to convey personal visions"; in "composing pastorals of similar designs"; and in the ways they "framed the outer world to give shape to the inner world."[35]

In *Winter, Monhegan Island* (1907), Kent rendered its western shore with other-worldly elements. He constructed a series of passages in various shades of blue; the result is representational but the arrangement becomes abstract when land, water, and sky, although distinct, flow into each other. The white glow at the top of the canvas suggests the presence of a force uniting all elements in the composition.

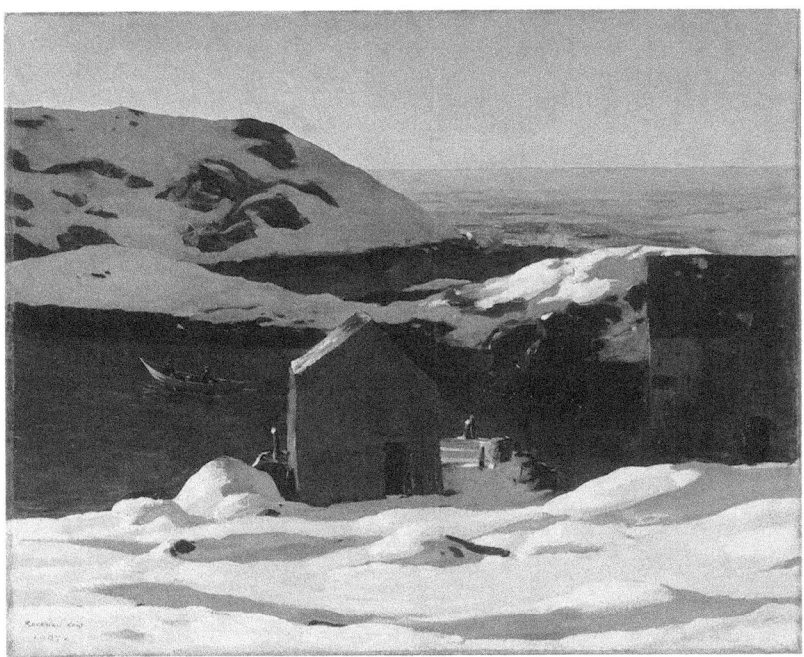

**Figure 3:** *Winter, Monhegan Island.* 1907. Oil on canvas. 86 × 118 cm. Metropolitans Museum of Art.

Forbes Watson of the *Evening Post* praised this canvas as "an exceptionally fine specimen" and noted that its "unfinished" nature [was] an affront to the academicians."[36] He was pointing out how the sharp abstract shapes of the building contrasted with the flowing lines of the snow, mountain and sky.

Kent's stay on Monhegan allowed him to stake his claim in the competitive world of American art. There, he honed his technical skills, redefined the possibilities of landscape painting, deepened his socialist convictions, embraced outdoor living, and forged what he hoped was a clear sense of himself as man and artist.

CHAPTER 4

# The "Self" and the "Better Self" (1908–1911)

In 1908, Kent's work was included *in Exhibition of Paintings and Drawings by Contemporary American Artists* at the Old Harmonie Club in Manhattan. His career was moving along—although slowly.

While staying at Dublin in January 1908, Kent met Thayer's niece Kathleen Whiting. His chivalrous, gentlemanly side was instantly drawn to this

> tall, shy, beautiful young girl of barely seventeen, [who] showed in her carriage and her quiet manner all premonitions, compatible with youth, of the true stateliness that was to grace her later womanhood. Deep-voiced, soft-spoken, gentle, she revealed the depths of her emotional nature only when, overcoming her shyness and her natural modesty, she would sing and play for us.[37]

Smitten, less than a month later, he traveled with Thayer's son Gerald—sharing Kent's horse, Kitty—to Crestalban, the Whiting farm in Lanesborough, Massachusetts in the Berkshires. The journey of 90 miles in severe weather took its toll on the two travelers. When he arrived, Kent's frostbite was so severe that he was immediately put to bed, where he was nursed by Kathleen. Their romance blossomed. They became engaged, although Kathleen's parents insisted the marriage take place only after she turned 18.

That spring Kent returned to Monhegan to complete work on his and his mother's house. To his own, he added a porch and a room. In October he visited his fiancée in the Berkshires. That was not a happy occasion. Familiarity between Kent and the Whitings bred contempt. They disapproved of Kent's unconventional views on socialism, the underclass, and his admiration for

## CHAPTER 4

Emerson, Thoreau and Whitman. When he encountered resistance, Kent could be obstreperous and confrontational. Concerned about their daughter's well-being, her parents insisted the couple spend the first year of their married life nearby. Kent took a drafting job in nearby Pittsfield. The marriage ceremony, on Kent's insistence, was a civil one.

That year, the newlyweds attended socialist meetings in Pittsfield and spent a week in New York City where they attended an opera every night. Kathleen looked forward to moving to Monhegan, where she could play the grand piano a neighbor had given to her husband. She was certain she could be happy there.

To better their precarious finances, the couple moved to Caritas Island, an island connected by bridge to Greenwich, Connecticut. At that time, the island was a hub of socialist activities. The couple's son—Rockwell III (Rocky)—was born there on October 25, 1909. Kent returned to work at Ewing and Chappell. As before, the commute was taxing, leaving him little time to paint. To stay connected with his art, he re-enrolled in Henri's night class at the New York School of Art. With the financial assistance of his mother, Kent founded the Monhegan Summer School of Art. Kathleen stayed back in Connecticut.

That summer was a turning point for Kent. His only prior sexual experience—likely an encounter with a prostitute—stood in sharp contrast to the reality of marriage. Two years of wedlock had shattered his youthful fantasies of bliss, leaving him to confront a painful truth.

> anticipation, aggravated, heightened by over-long deferment can breed hopes beyond all possible fulfillment. And that in me it did. And that as my young wife approached that inevitable and most moving metamorphosis of bride or mistress into motherhood, the particular bliss which I had so long and fervently awaited was dissolving even as I held it in my arms.[38]

That disappointment *seemed* to liberate him. During previous stays at Monhegan, he had developed a passionate but non-physical relationship with Jane Bell (Jennie) Sterling. He began "to wonder to what lengths it goes, how much of which you cherish as your secret, inner thoughts another has discerned. I wondered about *her*, plain, alluring little girl; and, wondering, I sensed sweet qualifies that drew me to her."[39] In 1903, when he arrived at

## THE "SELF" AND THE "BETTER SELF" (1908-1911)

Monhegan, Jennie would have been about 12 years old. By 1907, they had become a (Platonic) couple and by 1910 lovers.

Kent decided to confess to Kathleen "the triangle" he had built. "And in the quaint and disastrous illusion that it always best to tell the truth, I told."[40] He also revealed that his mother had nearly caught him and Jenny having sex. He added: "As I write this it doesn't seem tragic & it didn't then. It has been a very thrilling episode & very amusing—if only you could see it so."[41]

Kathleen failed to see any humor in the situation. She and Rocky went to stay with her parents in the Berkshires. Although Kathleen tried to forgive her errant husband, her parents felt that their worst fears about their son-in-law had been confirmed. Abbott and Gerald Thayer upbraided him.

In turn, he castigated the Thayers and accused them of "*self*-complacency and conceit" and informed his wife that she should choose between them and her husband: "You can ... stay in the pure, holy and spotless sanctuary of Thayerdom watched over by the immaculate flesh eater, the pure and lofty Abbott H. Thayer, or come to this stinking den of vice and degeneracy. But *don't* bring along any of that purity and virtue with you."[42] Although given little choice, Kathleen eventually chose her husband.

To explain and justify his conduct, Kent introduced a character into his autobiography that he called his "Better Self."

> the moment has arrived—and how reluctantly I welcome it!—to introduce a hitherto unmentioned member of our household, a young companion of exactly my own age and so closely resembling me in outward experience that, but for the sort of "Holier than thou" expresssion which distinguished him, we might have been—although we never were—mistaken for each other.[43]

The "Better Self" was less an alter ego than—in Freudian terms—the "super ego": the idealistic conscience that restrained impulsive desires. For Kent, the "Better Self" had been a fantasist whose concerns could now be cast aside by the "Self."

For Kent, the "Better Self" was a "damned, smug-faced interfering prig" with whom he had finally had a "reckoning." That character embodied the chivalry and gentility of a bygone era, which had "persistently worked on me throughout twenty-six years of my life, and delivered me almost, if not

CHAPTER 4

quite, unsullied and seemingly conditioned to everlasting virtue, at the altar of matrimony."[44]

Kent felt liberated when he shed the "Better Self" in favor of the "Self." This new person separated him from constricting societal conventions. In many ways, this was a liberating experience. He could become a man and artist of the twentieth century—one who had determinedly abandoned the mores of the nineteenth. He became prone to overriding the rights of others, provoking arguments, and denouncing opinions that did not match his own. Having once gone too far in one direction, he now did the same in the other.

A blend of the "Better Self" and the "Self" remained fixed in Kent's character. On a stroll one evening in about 1911 in Greenwich Village, Kent came upon a beautiful young woman whom, he noticed, was looking expectantly at various men. Intrigued, he approached her and suggested they walk together. They had strode a few paces when a policeman accosted them. The woman was arrested on suspicion of being a prostitute. Kent attended the night court where she was arraigned. There, he had a heated argument with the judge, who accused him of being the lady's pimp and ordered the woman to be held overnight. The next day, Kent appeared at the court to intercede on her behalf. A new judge, who possessed a more lenient nature, took Kent at his word that the lady had not propositioned him and let her go with a warning. Kent reflected: "I used often to wonder what became of [her]; I still wonder. For a time I reproached myself that I saw no more of her."[45]

This episode is complex and open to interpretation. Kent may have known full well the woman was a prostitute and intended to hire her. Yet, his "Better Self" surfaced when the two of them were stopped. In protecting her, he may have been assuaging his own sexual feelings and allowing his empathy with the marginalized to surface.

Kent's psychic conflicts are reflected in *Men and Mountains* (1909). Set against a spectacular setting in the Berkshires, naked men wrestle with each other. On the right, the pair recreate the traditional iconography of Hercules' celebrated defeat of the giant Antaeus. The sky above swirls with blue and white clouds in contrast with the brown plain on which the combat takes place. The opposing color schemes reflect the domain of each man.

THE "SELF" AND THE "BETTER SELF" (1908–1911)

In mythology, Antaeus represents the earth whereas Hercules is associated with the sky. Hercules won the encounter. Perhaps Kent was unconsciously stating that his new self was still rooted in the spirit, not the earth.

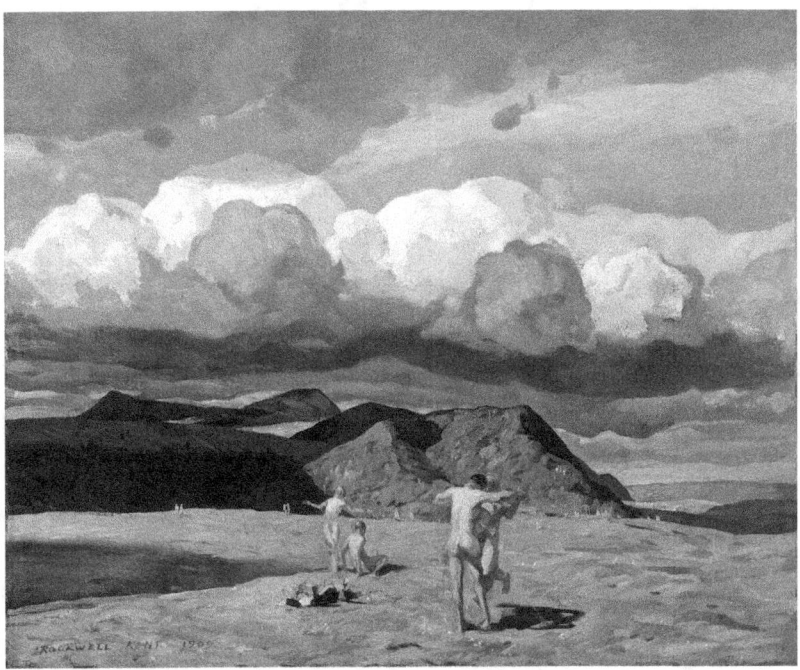

**Figure 4:** *Men and Mountains*. 1909. Oil on canvas. 83.8 × 109.8 cm. Columbus Museum of Art.

In 1910, Henri arranged to have this painting shown in a large show of modern American art in Columbus, Ohio. The painting offended the directors so deeply that they tried to ban it from the exhibition. Henri finally agreed to have the painting placed in a gallery marked "MEN ONLY."

CHAPTER 5

# Carpenter (1910–1913)

Ridding himself of his "Better Self," Kent hoped, would lead to psychic liberation. It did not work that way. While he may have cast away a great deal of self-imposed stress, he also unleashed that side of himself that was obdurate and blind to the needs of others. Before, there had been the "Self" and the "Better Self." He now became a person who tended to make decisions based solely on self-interest. Outwardly, he appeared dazzlingly self-assured; beneath that façade; however, he remained deeply conflicted.

Kent abandoned Monhegan, the place he had come into his own as a landscape painter. He may have done so to assure Kathleen he had severed himself from any temptations lingering there. On October 21, 1910, in search of a new location to facilitate his commitment to landscape painting, he traveled to Port aux Basques in Newfoundland and visited, among other places, Grand Bank and then Burin, a spot he considered a promising site for an art school.

On the way to Newfoundland, he stopped in Boston to catch the train for North Sydney, Nova Scotia, where he would board a boat to Newfoundland. He was aware that Jennie was living there. He called on her, and they dined together that evening. His "Better Self" restrained him—at first. But when he learned that there was no train for Nova Scotia the next day, he called on her again and spent the night with her in a hotel.

Upon arriving in Newfoundland, he had a heated quarrel with a customs officer who insisted upon charging him duty on his sketching materials as if they were photographic equipment. Outraged, Kent took the matter up with the Prime Minister of the Dominion, Sir Edward Morris, who by chance was visiting Port aux Basques. Morris settled the matter in Kent's favor and was intrigued by his proposal for an art school. On November 3,

CHAPTER 5

the two men met in St. John's. At that meeting, Morris promised support should Kent go ahead with establishing a school at Burin. That scouting mission lasted a month, in part because Kathleen pleaded with him to return home.

The already strained marriage broke open when Kent confessed to his wife that he had resumed his affair with Jennie in Boston. She had given birth to a son, Karl, in June 1911—two months after Kathleen had delivered a daughter, named Kathleen, born prematurely, on April 19, 1911. Moreover, Kent asked his wife if Jennie and Karl could join their household.

On October 11, 1911, Kathleen informed her husband: "You must leave me and go to Jennie! I can't ever be comfortable and happy with you, thinking how I am making her suffer. I can't be happy at the expense of someone else....If you absolutely refuse to do this for me, you must promise to sell my diamonds and economize in every possible way so that Jennie can keep Karl with her." She ended her letter with a declaration: she had to make "definite plans for myself."[46] Two days later, Kent responded: "I do not believe I could live if death or anything separated us." He then warned her: "Do not, unless you really want to ruin my life utterly, ever try to leave me." He added: "You cannot help Jennie by driving me off."[47]

When Jennie and Karl visited, Kathleen could not tolerate her presence and refused to acquiesce to a ménage à trois. As a compromise, the Kents decided to give their capital—four thousand dollars from the sale of the artist's Monhegan house—to the new mother. "And so, Kathleen," Kent told his wife, "we start all over again and this time really at scratch."[48]

Kent's financial situation in 1911 became grim. He worked intermittently for Ewing and Chappell. That April, together with Arthur B. Davies, he helped organize *An Independent Exhibition of the Paintings and Drawings of Twelve Men* at the Gallery of the Society of Beaux-Arts Architects.[49] He submitted 15 paintings and 24 drawings of Monhegan and the Berkshires. At the same time, Robert Henri and Harry Watrous curated a show at the Union League, also in New York, where Kent's work was also displayed. Nothing sold. In desperation, Kent offered 13, mainly Monhegan, paintings, to the dealer William Macbeth for five hundred dollars.

Using that money, Kent established what proved to be the short-lived New Hampshire School of Art in Richmond. Depressed but compelled to paint, he recalled: "Turning my back on reality, I struggled without conviction and, of course, without success in the composition of a strange variety of allegorical pictures that I may boast of having had the wisdom never to exhibit."[50] That October, the Kent family moved to 4 Perry Street in Greenwich Village.

Back in Manhattan, Kent's relationship with his former teacher Kenneth Hayes Miller was rekindled; he also became a close friend of the Maine-born artist Marsden Hartley, five years older than him. At that time, Kent resisted the mystical qualities in Miller's art and was likely aware of similar quasi-spiritual elements in Harley's landscapes. Though not yet ready to admit it, Kent shared more with them than he cared to acknowledge.

Kent was ready for a fresh start in a new place when he accepted a commission from the architectural firm of Lord, Hewlett and Tallent to oversee the construction of twin Georgian mansions in Winona, Minnesota. In the spring of 1912 the Kents moved to a place startlingly different from Greenwich Village. The small manufacturing town of 15,000 on the Mississippi was in the southern part of the state. The Kents rented a tiny abandoned schoolhouse near the building site. Kent opened an office in town and soon afterwards closed it because it failed to attracted any customers. To supplement his income, he sold fruit and vegetables from a wagon. He also acquired an obstreperous black gelding named John Brown after the abolitionist. On one occasion, the fiery animal threw his owner to the ground, shattered the family carriage, and left his owner with a broken arm.

While in Winona, Kent kept in touch with another Greenwich Village friend, the artist (William) Robert Pearmain, who had been born to a wealthy family in Dublin, New Hampshire. Even more ardent in his pursuit of social justice than Kent, Robert and his wife, Nancy, were members of the Industrial Workers of the World. He wrote to Kent:

> We don't care about becoming leaders, nor do we feel we are making any sacrifice, because we believe the workers (the skilled and unskilled) are the most deserving of the people and the finest, and we think it best to throw in our lot with them, taking their trials, suffering, and persecutions along with them as mere individuals and joining them in the great fight for freedom.[51]

## CHAPTER 5

True to his word, Pearmain took work at a Westinghouse plant. From childhood, he had experienced frail health; his body could not bear the strain to which he subjected it. He died on September 8, 1912, at the age of 24. That death shook Kent.

Since he was not hesitant to share political opinions anathematic to most of the townspeople in Winona, he and his family lived under threat—rocks were thrown through their windows and the water pipes to the schoolhouse destroyed. In addition to these difficulties, Kathleen was again pregnant. She decided to move back to New York for the baby's birth—Clara was born on June 30, 1913.

Kent remained behind. He joined the local union and worked as a laborer on the buildings whose construction he was overseeing. The local newspaper ran this headline: PAINTER OF FAME WORKS AS CARPENTER. When his construction team demanded higher wages, Kent acted as their spokesman. A strike ensued before work was resumed on the houses.

During his absence in Winona, the *International Exhibition of Modern Art*—the Armory Show—opened in New York in February 1913. Duchamp's daring, experimental *Nude Descending a Staircase* may have mercilessly mocked in the press, but this exhibition introduced a host of new modernisms to America, including Cubism. His own take on modernism, Kent believed, "accepted the traditional *language* of art and aimed at nothing but its purification and re-invigoration through the elimination of sentimental clichés" but it also aimed "to secure to all artists ... freedom of expression."[52] For Kent, Cubism led to "the sterile, dead-end byways of abstractionism."[53]

When Kent returned to New York after his stay in the Midwest, the art world had shifted in new and—to what seemed to him—outlandish ways. He resumed working for Ewing and Chappell, but he remained at loose ends. A deus ex machina emerged when Charles Daniel became his dealer. The gallery on West 47th Street, showcased artists of Kent's avant-garde persuasion.

Still dissatisfied with life in New York and anxious to find a new path, Kent considered returning to Newfoundland. He took matters in hand when he asked Daniel to pay him $200 a month in exchange for exclusive rights to his work. Daniel was hesitant, committed himself, and then backed out. Sara Kent pledged $50 a month. With that modest support, Kent decided to abandon New York in pursuit of a new landscape.

Marsden Hartley was skeptical of his friend's decision to find "solace in Newfoundland among lost and forsaken things—wastelands and thoughtless seas—and a vastness of diffident nature generally." He believed that such a refuge was not sufficient "for a young mind and a soul eager for life." Hartley's prediction would prove wrong. Newfoundland transformed Kent's art.

CHAPTER 6

# Expatriate (1914–1915)

On February 25, 1914, Kent, after four days at sea, arrived in St. John's. He had originally planned to return to Burin but that place did not really suit him. Upon advice from locals, he decided to settle in Brigus, 40 miles from St. John's on Conception Bay. He considered staying in a decaying Georgian mansion but sensibly chose a "little house on a narrow shelf or terrace, that had been dug from the steep hillside bordering the bay."[54] The interior badly needed attention. He renovated the two rooms upstairs, the two downstairs. He even added a cubby-hole for an easel and a chair. The gloom of winter was lifted by the arrival of Kathleen and their three children. In those cramped quarters, Kathleen gave birth to their fourth child, Barbara, on June 16, 1915, and then spent several weeks in hospital in St. John's recuperating.

That winter brought tragedy to the Dominion. The S.S. *Southern Cross* was lost with 176 men aboard, some from Brigus. Another disaster claimed the lives of 78 sealers from the S.S. *Newfoundland*. Kent joined his neighbors in mourning those losses. Through his friendship with the head of the Fishermen's Protective Union, he became involved in local issues and published two short essays supporting that group.

Kent could be deeply altruistic but when he felt his rights were quashed, he responded with extreme aggression—sometimes proudly so. While helping to establish the Brigus Tennis Club, he became outraged when the landowner objected to it being turned into a court. Kent ordered the landowner off the property. Subsequently, Kent waylaid this individual, collared him in the neck and hurled a barrage of insults at him. Not surprisingly, the victim reported the incident. At the trial, the judge asked Kent if he had threatened to kill this person. Yes, he answered—and added that he had also threatened to eat

## CHAPTER 6

him. Kent was found guilty, paid the fine, and boasted: "And so ended the great *Case of the Assaulted Apothecary*."[55]

Another brouhaha erupted when the Great War began in August 1914. Since childhood, Kent had been a Germanophile. In Brigus, he spoke openly of his pro-German sympathies. In Newfoundland, at that time a Dominion of the British Empire, hostility toward the enemy ran high. Kent then became involved in what he called "the momentous and consequential *Case of the German Spy of Brigus*."[56]

Rumors began circulating that Kent was not American but a German spy. Undeterred, Kent added fuel to the fire by painting a German eagle on a board outside his workshop. On August 31, a constable and a detective sergeant called on him to assess his nationality. Four days later, he was interviewed in St. John's and, when that meeting went badly, he appealed to the American Consul to intercede with the Prime Minister. Nothing happened. Undeterred, Kent published a piece in December 1914 in the St. John's *The Mail and Advocate*: "Spy Scare Strikes Brigus." The following May Kent expressed his disgust at the "dismal little British colony" of Newfoundland.[57] In mid-July 1915, he and his family were ordered to leave, which they did on July 31.

In *It's Me O Lord*, although three chapters are devoted to 1914 and 1915 in Newfoundland, Kent said little about life there as an artist apart from one revealing aside:

> Yet to any pretense that my prevailing mood in wartime Newfoundland was one of cheer, my paintings give the lie. Compelled, by the nature of the weather and the difficulty going far afoot, to work indoors and in the narrow confines of my studio, forced to reflect and, by reflection, thrown upon the harsh realities of a war-torn world, my work was in no way an outpouring of delight in visible nature but, rather, a continuous wail of lamentation of man's tragic, solitary lot in the vast and soulless cosmos. The war, the senseless sacrifice of lives, the hatred war engendered, and, on us, the foul suspicions so at variance with our true, innate integrity: these facts oppressed me to a degree to which I only let my work give utterance.[58]

In this startling passage—at odds with the other information he provided about his stay in Newfoundland—he admitted that he had endured deep anguish during that time. Although he referred to his distress at being suspected of treason as a contributing factor, he attributed his dark feelings to his distress about the brutality and senselessness of war.

This statement cannot be accepted at face value because it leaves essential questions unanswered. First, Kent's violent behavior and pro-German antics may have come into play as a distraction from depressed feelings. Second, His distress might have extended to uneasy feelings about his marriage: living in confined quarters in Brigus may have exacerbated the already precarious relationship between husband and wife. Third, Kent tended to express anxious feelings in images rather than words. The Newfoundland paintings—so different from his previous work—provided him with the opportunity to explore that inner turmoil.

Before leaving Newfoundland, Kent told his dealer Charles Daniel that his recent work contained a "distinct spiritual message ... utterly different from anyone's."[59] This variance is striking and can be seen when comparing *Down to the Sea* (1910) from Monhegan to *Burial of a Young Man* (1911) from Kent's first stay in Newfoundland.

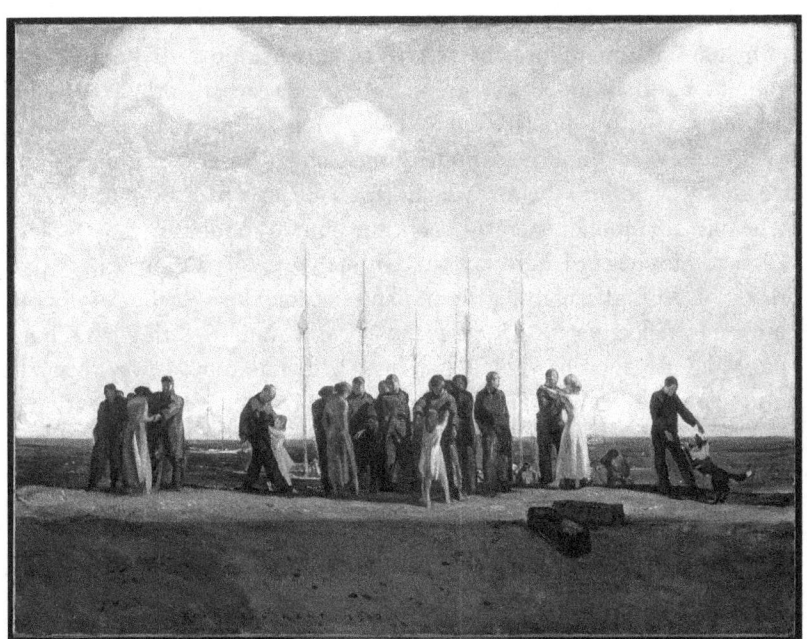

**Figure 5:** *Down to the Sea*. 1910. Oil on canvas. 108 × 142.9 cm. Brooklyn Museum.

# CHAPTER 6

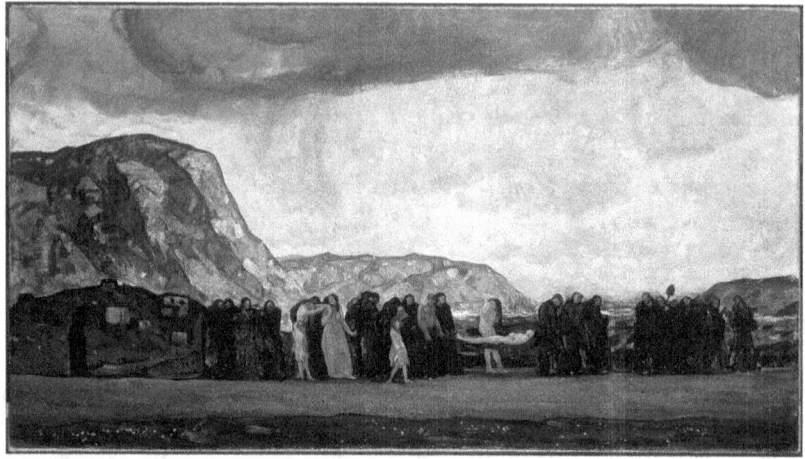

**Figure 6:** *Burial of a Young Man*. c. 1908–1911. Oil on canvas. 71 × 133 cm. Phillips Collection.

Both share a similar three-part vertical composition—sky, figures, and ground—but their mood diverges sharply. In the earlier work, women and children mournfully bid farewell to the seafarers against a cloudy yet bright sky. In *Burial*, the mourners, under a menacing dark-gray sky, merge into one another and into the rocky landscape. The later painting turns a local scene into a symbolic statement about the human condition.

Kent's Monhegan landscapes were in many ways traditional; his works during his second stay in Newfoundland became dreamscapes—symbolic landscapes reflecting his private fears. This shift aligns with what scholar Jake Milgram Wien has noted as Kent's deliberate move "away from the naturalism of his early years towards a more introspective interpretation of land and sea."[60]

In the spring of 1911, as mentioned above, Kent had co-organized *An Independent Exhibition of the Paintings and Drawings of Twelve Men* with Arthur B. Davies, who admired and was inspired by Symbolist painters like Ferdinand Hodler, William Blake, Puvis de Chavannes, and Albert Pinkham Ryder, artists who, in various ways incorporated symbols in their work. Kent may well have been influenced by those artists beginning in 1914-5.

Before his second stay in Newfoundland, Kent's modernism followed that of Robert Henri and the Ashcan School. The Brigus paintings reflect an intimate knowledge of European Symbolism. Although Kent remained a fierce opponent of Cubism and other forms of abstract art, he was not averse to other types of modernist art, particularly Nordic or German ones. Before he arrived in Newfoundland in 1914—as mentioned above—he had begun painting in an allegorical manner. His previous landscapes were underpopulated; the new ones depict anguished men and women reminiscent of Munch; in one, a stag-like creature evokes Franz Marc and the *Der Blaue Reiter* circle. Some use colors as intense as Gauguin's.

In *Pastoral* (1914), dark blues and greens frame a mourning figure and a stag. *The House of Dread* (c. 1914–1917), with its stage-like composition, echoes the despair of Ibsen and Strindberg. In *Newfoundland Dirge* (c. 1914–1917), figures are embedded in the land itself. *A Young Sailor* (c. 1914–1917) bears the haunting gaze of a Munch figure.

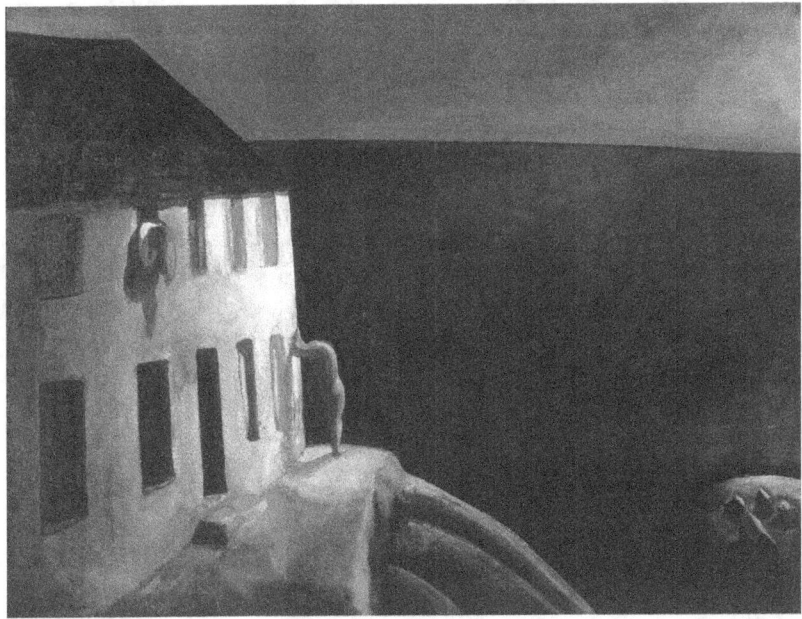

**Figure 7:** *The House of Dread*. c. 1914–1917. Oil on canvas. 70.5 × 95.9 cm. Plattsburgh State Art Museum.

## CHAPTER 6

These paintings may memorialize communal tragedies. Yet they also reveal private despair and are intimate expressions of dejection and hopelessness. This is particularly true of *The House of Dread*, which exposes the emotional distance between Kathleen and her husband. The anguished woman at the top of the house is separated from the grief-stricken man below. Both are angst-ridden, but they may not be experiencing the same sorrows.

In reflecting what he accomplished in Newfoundland, Kent told Daniel: "I do literally transport myself into the land that with my own pigment I create: painting has become for me the act of populating the realms that I build and that appear to me so splendid ... I must confess to you that I am coming to realize, or to believe, that I have a distinct spiritual message that is utterly different from anyone's and is moreover well worthwhile. I begin to see what I stand for."[61] The critic Charles Caffin observed that Kent's new reliance on human figures displayed "rude, organic structures, with exaggerations and distortions of form, like the nature out of which they have grown." He also praised the "conflicts of discord rather than the agreement of harmony" in Kent's use of color.[62]

Not all the symbolist paintings are grim. Daniel told Kent that he considered *Portrait of a Child* (*My Daughter Clara*) (c. 1914) "a genuine work, something dug out of yourself, and of which one could paraphrase Whitman and say 'this is not a picture, it is the man.'"[63] The sleeping infant—perhaps inspired by the series of images of mystical babies by the German artist Philipp Otto Runge—lies peacefully in the natural world, although the somber background hints at life's challenges.

Kent's second stay in Newfoundland was emotionally draining. Yet that experience forced him to confront himself and opened a path to new artistic expression—transforming his landscapes into symbolic meditations on resilience and fragility.

EXPATRIATE (1914–1915)

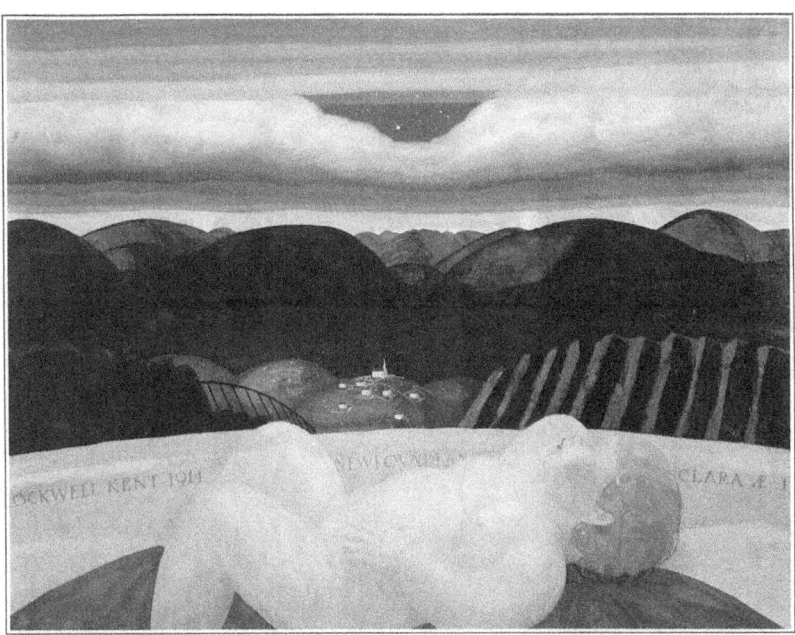

**Figure 8:** *Portrait of a Child (My Daughter Clara)*. 1914. Oil on canvas. 54 × 72 cm. Pushkin State Museum of Fine Arts.

## Chapter 7

# Satirist (1915–1918)

Upon his return from Newfoundland in 1915, Kent wanted to expand the new directions he had taken in his art. He also needed to support himself and his family. George Chappell rehired him and that summer settled the Kents in a cottage in New London, Connecticut. In Manhattan, Charles Daniel arranged for Kent, when in the city, to stay at the studio of the Canadian-born painter, Edward Middleton Manigault, a former classmate at the New York School of Art.

House prices in Manhattan were too expensive for Kent's limited means, so that autumn he bought a house on Staten Island (1262 Richmond Terrace, West Brighton) with an arbor and plenty of land. Unfortunately, the stench from a factory on the Jersey shore prevented the Kents from enjoying their new home.

The family remained there until the spring of 1917 when the United States entered World War I. The resulting economic slump left no work for Kent at Ewing and Chappell. To save money, the Staten Island house was sold. Kathleen and the children moved to Sara Kent's house on Monhegan, and Kent, in hope of obtaining freelance work, rented a utility apartment (a room with bath) on 23 West Twelfth Street in Greenwich Village.

Kent was elated when the distinguished architect Henry Hornbostel hired him to make renderings for him. Kent made all kinds of drawings of huge buildings that "bore some kinship to those elemental forms of nature that I loved: mountains and bare rocks." His employer informed him that he "could

CHAPTER 7

suit [his] work hours to suit [his] own convenience ... There was a job after my own heart; I accepted it, and went to work." That scheme collapsed when Kent learned that Hornbostel had no intention of paying him a semblance of an acceptable wage. After his final encounter with him, Kent wrote the architect a letter of which he kept no copy. "And Henry Hornbostel," he gloated, "I am quite sure, did not keep his."[64]

More reliable work became available. Soon after returning from Newfoundland, Kent provided drawings to *Harper's Weekly*. From February to May 1916, he drew portraits of celebrities such as Charlie Chaplin and John D. Rockefeller for an eight part series entitled, "Plutarch Lights of History." Jake Wien has noted Kent's skill in blending contemporary with historical themes and employing a visual vocabulary of wide-ranging allusions. "His versatility made him equally at home depicting baseball diamond and movie house."[65] Then, unfortunately, that magazine folded.

Earlier, in 1913, Kent had supplied the illustrations for Fredrick Squires' *Architec-tonics*—a book that poked fun at fellow architects. Later, George Chappell invited Kent to illustrate 12 satirical essays by him for *The Bricklayer*, a monthly magazine for architects. When *Harper's* ceased publication, Kent recalled Chappell's verses about Manhattan high life that he had published from time to time in *Vanity Fair*. In Kent's opinion, they cried out for illustrations. He prepared a portfolio and called upon Frank Crowninshield, the magazine's editor, who was immediately taken with the selection and purchased several on the spot. But, the editor lamented, the drawings were not signed. Kent pointed out that he was a serious artist and did not wish his name to be associated with frivolities. Crowninshield retorted that the artist could do as he wished, so Kent adopted the pseudonym: "Wm. Hogarth, Jr." And so, as Kent put it, "his 'unworthy namesake'" was launched.[66]

Kent's drawings lured him into a world with which he was only vaguely familiar but to which he quickly became a habitué. Wien has argued that Kent's work for that magazine "reflect[ed] a new-found fascination with high fashion and its elite European magazines." Crowninshield urged him to employ "attenuation and grace" and insisted that his women be "thin and long and very silly."[67]

# SATIRIST (1915–1918)

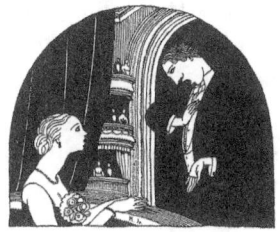
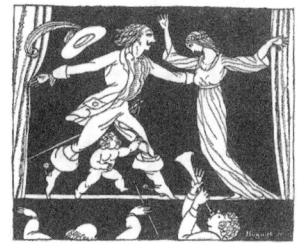
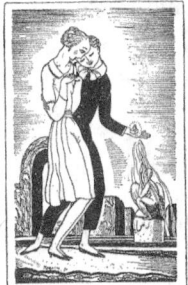
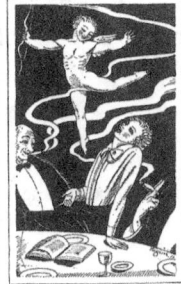
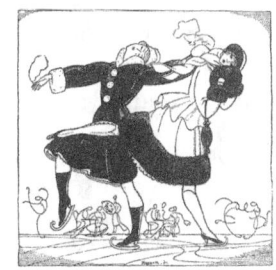
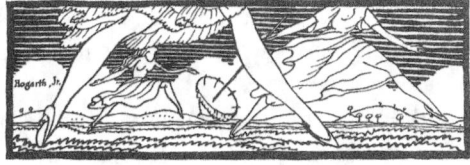
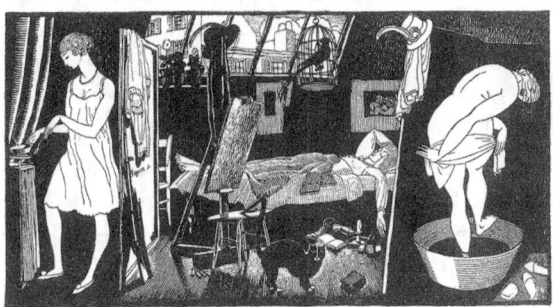

**Figure 9:** Drawings by "Hogarth, Jr." for *Vanity Fair*, *Puck* and *A Basket of Poses*. 1915–1924.

## CHAPTER 7

Kent's success at *Vanity Fair* led to regular work from other magazines—among them, *Puck* and *Judge*. Before these commissions, he had been nearly broke; now, modest prosperity seemed possible. Still, he felt conflicted, describing the work as "slick and commercial ... Oh God—that a man should at thirty-five—with all the wisdom and brains that I have—be making these fool things!"[68]

Just as he was drawn into a milieu vastly different from his own, Kent became involved with a woman utterly unlike Kathleen or Jennie. His first encounter with Hildegarde Hirsch, a dancer in the Ziegfeld Follies, was overpowering. He was standing at the corner of Forty-fifth Street and Seventh Avenue where he observed a young woman.

> And as, with it being the month of June [1916] ... what with her being so prettily dressed in white and it so well becoming her golden hair, red lips, blue eyes, what with my being me, it suddenly came over me that never in all my life had I seen so entrancingly lovely a creature.

He realized that if he had still been under the influence of his "late lamented Better Self" that "would have been the end of our little story. But I wasn't. Suddenly it flashed upon me what a boob I was to stand and watch her walking off."[69]

He caught up with Hildegarde and a mad swirl ensued. Two weeks later, they took a train to Peterborough, New Hampshire where they pitched a tent. Thirty-five years later, Kent felt he could devote a book to the following week: "we had no sense of guilt; and like Eve and Adam following their fall, could abandon ourselves to the enjoyment of every pleasure that the body and the soul of man might crave."[70]

Hildegarde, who was born and raised in Munich, was 28 and divorced. She had traveled to the States as a member of a touring dance troupe. At some point she had been living with her sister, Frieda, also a dancer. By the summer of 1917, she was installed at her lover's Greenwich Village flat and so Kent was maintaining two households—one in Maine, one in Manhattan. On one occasion, Kent visited Hildegarde backstage at the Follies and wrote to Kathleen: "It was a great support and of course thrilling to be the center of attraction for so many beauties."[71]

## SATIRIST (1915–1918)

One bond between the lovers was German. He had spoken that language as a young child and felt a strong affinity with that country and its culture. He dreamed that he and Hildegarde would "have three children Tristan, Siegfried and Frieda, as beautiful as Rockwell, Kathleen, Clara and Hildegarde." (The fourth child's name was Barbara, but Kent referred to her as "little Hildegarde.")

Kent was a jealous lover, one easily riled when he felt Hildegarde was flirting with other men. He told her that his jealousy arose because of his low self-esteem. He also admitted to her that he was excessively self-centered. His love for Hildegarde was far more encompassing than what he had experienced with either Kathleen or Jennie. He once told Hildegarde that under her guidance he was growing in wisdom. "I pray so fervently that nature, if there were no God, would, for very pity, make one to hear me and to bless us both." For Kent, Hildegarde obviously existed in an entirely different sphere from any woman he had known. She was part of sophisticated Manhattan high life whereas he associated Kathleen and Jennie with the domestic and the rural.

Kent made many drawings of Kathleen that expressed tenderness and devotion, but they are devoid of the fervid sexuality and voluptuousness in which he rendered Hildegarde in some experiments with oil on glass (reverse painting), where her sexual allure glows. For Christmas 1916, he wrote and illustrated *The Jewel: A Romance of Fairyland* in which a prince and maiden make plans to escape to "Hildegarten," a dream house carpeted with moss and filled with flowers. The following year he gave her *The Jewel Box* accompanied by lock and key. The lid contained a polychrome, gilded relief with a reclining nude combing her luxuriant tresses.

In the midst of making his drawings for various magazines and at the height of his infatuation with Hildegarde, Kent did not neglect marketing his "serious" art and re-entering the art world he had abandoned while in Newfoundland. In February-March 1917, he exhibited Newfoundland canvases at the Daniel Gallery. The following April and May, he showed two canvases in the first annual *Exhibition of the American Society of Independent Artists*.

That unorthodox event was held in the 13 storey Grand Central Palace, at that time Manhattan's principal exhibition hall. As the show's full-time

## CHAPTER 7

organizer, he oversaw two thousand entries; the premise of the exhibition was contained in its motto: "No jury, no prizes, exhibits hung in alphabetical order." He recalled: "for the first, and happily, the last time in my life, [I] became a business executive."[72] Marcel Duchamp's *Fountain* was rejected for technical reasons, and, later, when the event's committee refused to pay its debts, Kent resigned.

In retrospect, Kent considered the most "propitious" moment in his life as an artist from 1915 to 1918 was his encounter with Marie Sterner, who was in charge of contemporary art at M. Knoedler & Co., one of the oldest and most prestigious commercial art galleries in the United States. In putting together an exhibition, she had come upon Kent's work and asked Charles Daniel if she could include a work of Kent's in her exhibition. Daniel refused. Undeterred, she approached Robert Henri to inquire if he would allow her to borrow a canvas Kent had given to him. The ever generous Henri told his former pupil: "Put a price on it and if it sells, the money shall, of course, be yours." Kent placed a low price on it whereupon Sterner sold it to the Metropolitan Museum of Art; in that transaction, Kent received double his asking price. Elated with that sale, Sterner asked Daniel if they could collaborate in marketing Kent's work. When he declined, Sterner became the artist's dealer. Well versed in placing art, in 1918 she sold a Newfoundland painting to Henry Clay Frick.

Suddenly on the verge of financial success, Kent determined to travel in pursuit of new landscapes. He even considered an offer to subsidize his traveling expenses to the Southwest by Southern Pacific Railway, but he was not attracted to the idea of a hot, sunny locale. His inclination was to paint a place, like Newfoundland, associated with the sea and cold weather. With the backing of some influential friends he obtained funds for traveling expenses to the Alaskan Territory (now Alaska).

Traveling arrangements were more than a little confused. Kent asked Kathleen, who was well aware of her husband's affair with Hildegarde, to accompany him on this expedition. She stated the obvious—she could not abandon four children. Then Kent implored Kathleen to allow nine-year Rocky to travel with him: "I can't face the thought of the loneliness I'm going into." Kathleen responded: "I wish you and Hilda would go but leave Rocky with me. It seems strange to me to think you are taking him away from me without my consent, after my plainly stating I did not want him to go."

She didn't care if he took Hildegarde, she assured him, "for I realize that she will always be a part of your life and that I must have a husband with a sweetheart or not have him at all." Eventually, she allowed Rocky to accompany his father. At this point, Kent must have felt that he could separate himself emotionally from both women.

In many ways, the journey to Alaska made little financial or personal sense. Kent was on the cusp of financial well-being. Marie Sterner had taken him on as a client. He was involved with the woman he considered the love of his life. Yet Kent's decision revealed where his true passion lay: in his art and the pursuit of his career as an artist. Conflicted as he was in his emotional life, Kent was most himself in that role.

CHAPTER 8

# Survivor (1918–1919)

Kent and Rocky boarded the westbound Canadian Pacific train to Vancouver in late July 1918. From British Columbia they continued to Seattle, where they took a ship to Juneau, Alaska. During the voyage, Kent wrote to Hildegarde, and that September—some weeks after arriving—he invited her to join him and Rocky in their new setting. He suggested she identify herself as his wife, or perhaps as his sister.

This was a precarious proposition, but it reveals how deeply the separation from Hildegarde had affected him. When she declined, Kent wrote to her three months later:

> I have chosen to go back to Kathleen and to the children, to leave New York and leave it forever maybe and go far into the country, somewhere where no other people will be, to live on the least it can be done for and dedicate my time to work without end. I do this of my own free will. I have no defense. I have not been urged or threatened by Kathleen of whose love I am far from being certain.[73]

This declaration may have marked a genuine change of heart—or served as an ultimatum. In any case, despite some later exchange of letters, the affair ended. Kent's overture to Hildegarde, followed by his break with her, suggests that Alaska heightened his emotional fragility. There, he would experience alternating waves of despair and exhilaration.

On August 24, father and son reached Seward, where they encountered photographer John E. Thwaites, who had spent much of his life documenting life in Alaska. Learning that Kent sought a tranquil place to work, Thwaites recommended Fox Island in Resurrection Bay, where a deserted cabin stood.

## CHAPTER 8

On the way to the island, the motor on their eighteen-foot dory, loaded with one hundred pounds of supplies, failed. The island's sole inhabitant, Lars Olson—an elderly Swede who kept angora goats and raised blue foxes—towed them ashore and welcomed their company. The island's three inhabitants, representing three generations, worked energetically to restore the cabin. Olson's deep knowledge of isolated living was invaluable; Rocky instinctively adapted to his surroundings— "his life was full: he made and it kept it so," his father boasted.[74] Kent, for his part, had found what he sought: a physically demanding environment that re-energized his art.

> It was for us to discover that quietude was not only compatible with adventure but might contribute to its very essence to which the more active, or at times exciting episodes served as mere foils to deepen our appreciation of the blessedness of the prevailing peace.[75]

Although previously resistant to mystical approaches to painting, such an inclination had surfaced in Newfoundland. Kent now became more receptive:

> I think that whatever of the mystic is in a man is essentially inseparable from him; it is his by the grace of God. After all, the qualities by which all of us become known are those of which we are ourselves least conscious. The best of me is what is quite impulsive, and looking at myself for a moment with a critic's eye, the forms that occur in my art, the gestures, the spirit of the whole of it, is in fact nothing but an exact pictorial record of an unconscious living idealism.[76]

He also altered his working method, as he told his friend Carl Zigrosser:

> During the daylight I paint by nature by way of fixing the forms and above all the color of the out of doors on my mind. Then, after dark, I go into a trance for a while with Rockwell subdued into absolute silence. I lie down or sit with closed eyes until I see a composition, then I make a quick note of it or maybe given an hour's time to perfecting the arrangement at a small scale.[77]

Zigrosser, of Austrian descent and a Columbia graduate, was then editor of *The Modern School*, a libertarian educational journal to which Kent contributed both text and art. A devoted supporter of the artist, Zigrosser introduced him to Coomaraswamy, Nietzsche, and Blake. Kent confessed that he was a *tabula rasa*: "You speak of mysticism. I have never been quite sure of what it meant [but] I have no contradictory beliefs to hamper the expression of my natural and undirected vision."[78]

Kent had long been drawn to Tolstoy's view that the artist has a duty to reveal the divine underpinnings of human existence. Nietzsche and Blake went further, asserting that divinity resided within the artist, whose role was to awaken in others the latent powers they rarely explored. The Ceylonese metaphysician Ananda Coomaraswamy, Kent noted, "defines mysticism as a belief in the unity of life. The creed of an artist concerns us only when we mean by it the tendency of his spirit."[79]

In Newfoundland, Kent had imbued his landscapes with symbolist elements. In Alaska, his work underwent a radical transformation toward simplification and purification. Sky and mountains became archetypes, not mere depictions. Elements were set in stark, dramatic opposition. In *Alaska Winter* (1919), the remains of a dead tree seem to have defiantly returned to life. In *Resurrection Bay—Alaska (Blue and Gold)* (1919) and *Resurrection Bay* (1919), the interplay of color heightens the symbolic force of the forms, achieved without human presence.

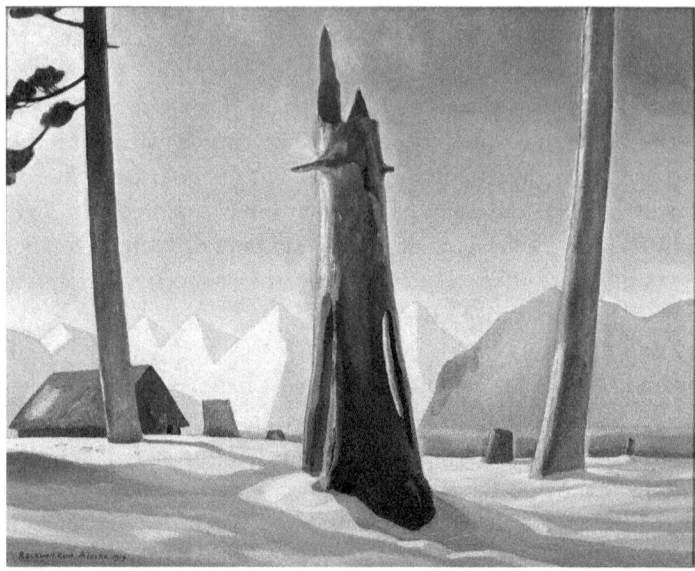

**Figure 10:** *Alaska Winter*. 1919. Oil on canvas. 86 × 110 cm. Anchorage Museum.

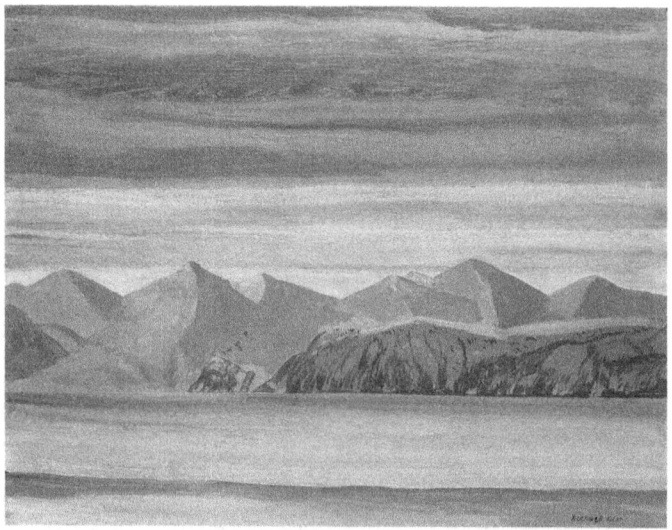

**Figure 11:** *Resurrection Bay, Alaska (Blue and Gold)*. 1919. 30 × 38 cm. Bowdoin College.

*North Wind* (1919), recalls his earlier symbolism. Against a blue and gray landscape, a youth in red, brown, and yellow strides across mountaintops, "reaching upward to embrace all space. About him are the stars. ... On the dark mountainous land beneath him men are living as they do to-day, with slaughter and the burning of homes."[80] The figure embodies the awakening to spiritual truth and the urge to share it.

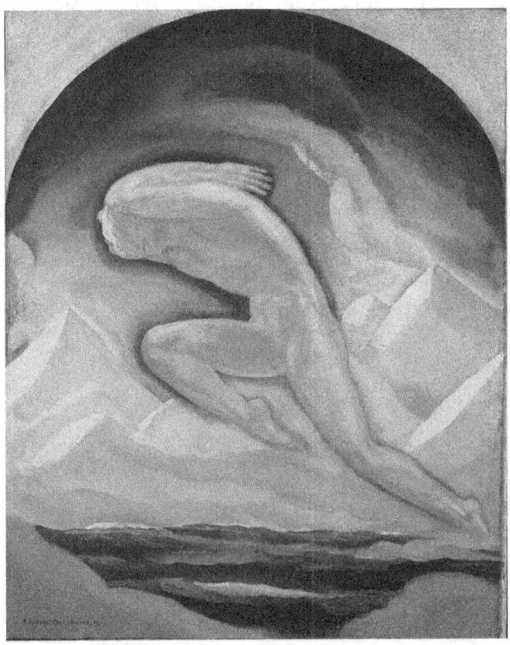

**Figure 12:** *North Wind.* 1919. Oil on canvas mounted on hardboard. 104 × 86 cm. The Phillips Collection.

This transformation is evident in *Wilderness: A Journal of Quiet Adventure in Alaska* (1920). The text narrates his arrival in Alaska, his establishment on Fox Island, the hardships of isolated living, the daily routines of father and son, and Kent's spiritual awakening. The frontispiece shows Rocky reclining at a cliff's edge, gazing toward the horizon. The dedication reads: "To old L.M. Olson and young Rockwell Kent of Fox Island this journal is respectfully dedicated."

## CHAPTER 8

The book's 46 pen, brush, and ink illustrations echo the events of the text, but also deepen and extend them. Some show Fox Island's landscapes (*Rain Torrents*), others depict Kent's labor to tame the land (*Home Building*), or father-and-son moments (*On the Height*). There are Nietzsche-inspired visions of renewal (*Superman*) alongside images of desolation (*Wilderness*) and the group images later titled "The Mad Hermit" (*Immanence*).

In his Alaskan landscapes, Kent rendered sea, land, and mountains in nearly abstract, monumental forms—forces locked in dynamic interplay. The *Wilderness* landscapes are more documentary, recording Fox Island's physical reality. But the figure compositions move far beyond that. They show the strenuous physical labor of settlement, the intimacy of father and son, and Kent's meditation on the loss of his own father—symbolized by the flute he carried. In the dedication image, Rocky embraces Olson, a gesture mirrored in Kent's narrative: "I've never dreamed of so sweet a disposition as he has shown to have. He's touchingly sensitive and kind; loves every living thing to the very gnat that stings him."[81]

# SURVIVOR (1918–1919)

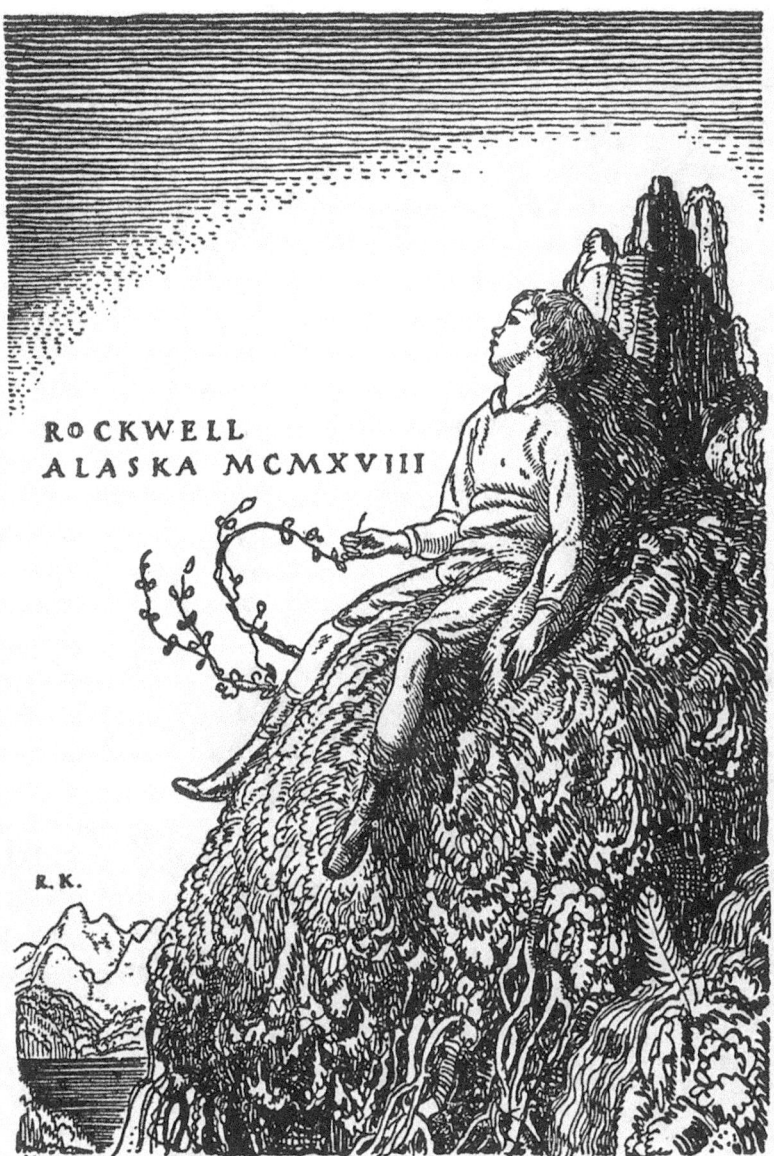

**Figure 13:** Frontispiece. *Wilderness*. 1920. Private Collection.

SURVIVOR (1918–1919)

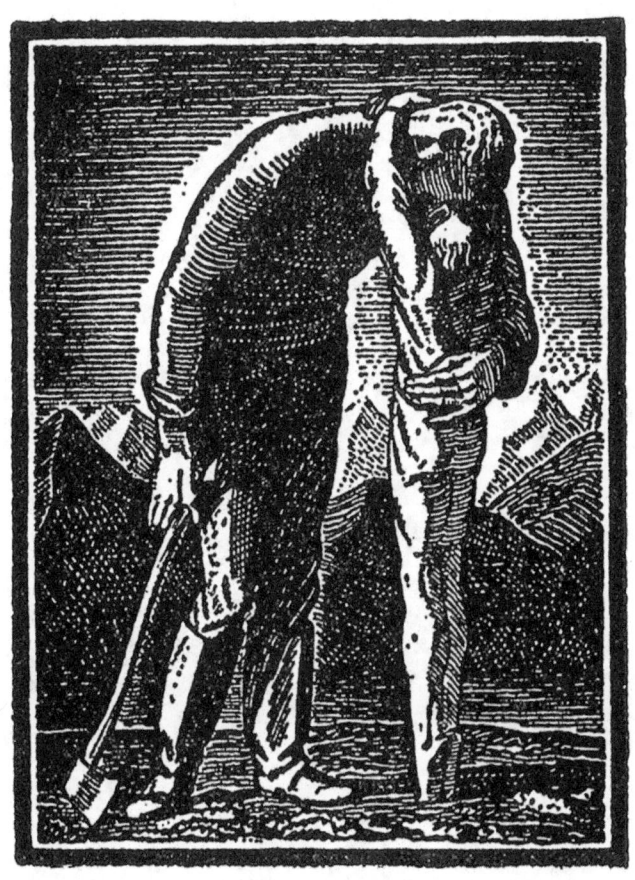

To old L. M. Olson and young Rockwell Kent of Fox Island this journal is respectfully dedicated

**Figure 14:** Dedication Page. *Wilderness*. 1920. Private Collection.

SURVIVOR (1918–1919)

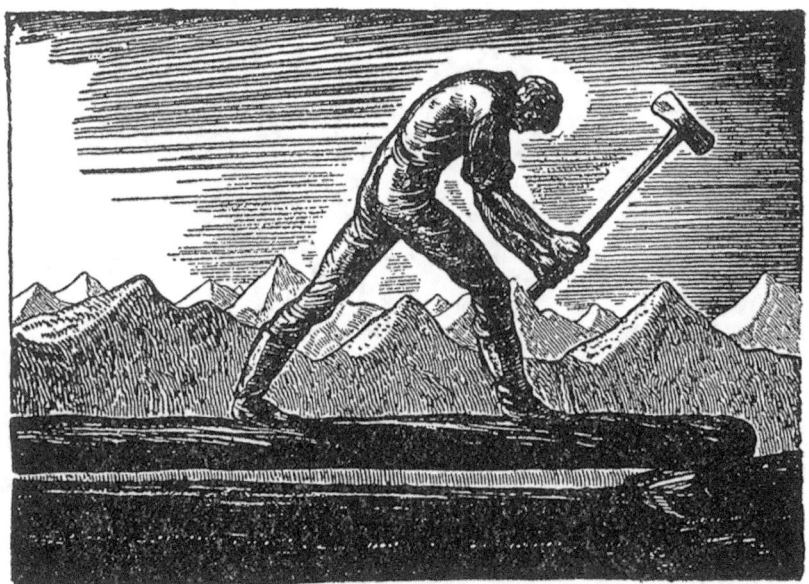

HOME BUILDING

**Figure 15:** *Home Building. Wilderness.* 1920. Private Collection.

SURVIVOR (1918–1919)

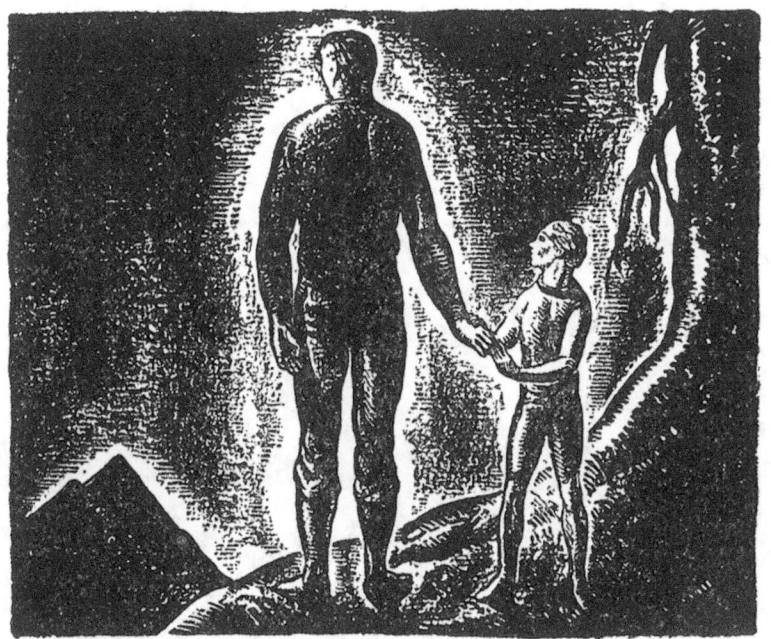

ON THE HEIGHT

**Figure 16:** *On the Height. Wilderness.* 1920. Private Collection.

SURVIVOR (1918–1919)

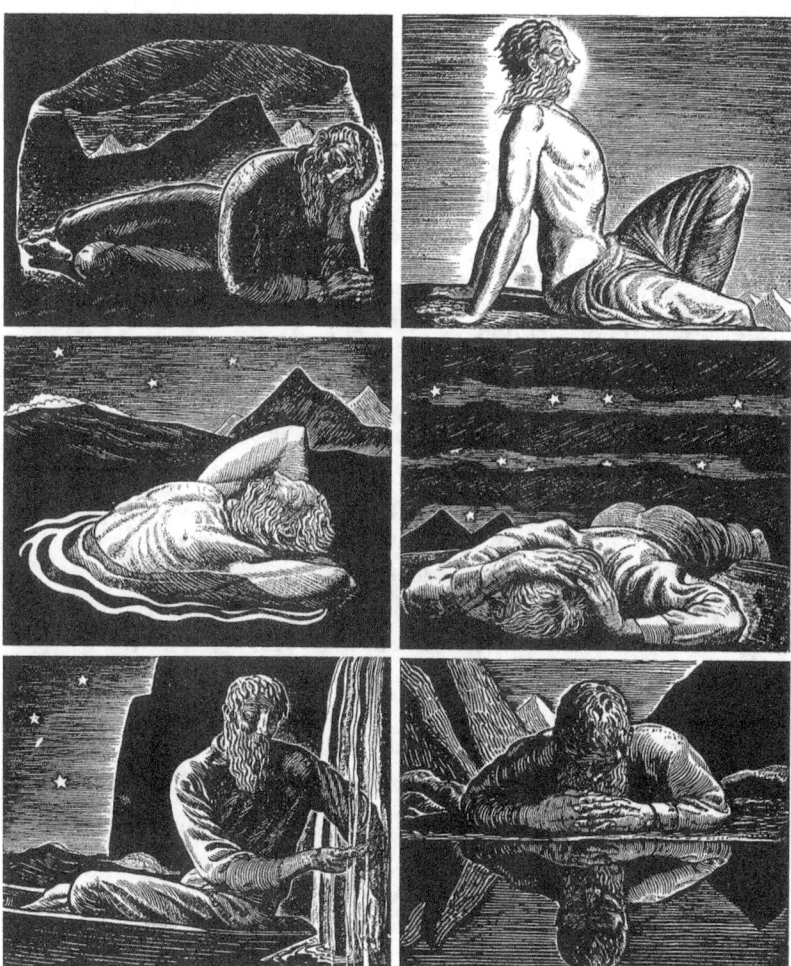

**Figure 17:** *The Mad Hermit. Wilderness.* 1920. Private Collection.

CHAPTER 8

Half the illustrations do not correspond directly to the text but chart stages in Kent's search for spiritual liberation. Those inspired by Nietzsche cast the artist as a Superman, liberating others through art; others express anxiety, melancholy, and the search for redemption. The "Mad Hermit" images—later grouped together—echo Blake's engravings for *The Book of Job*, in which God permits Satan to test Job. Like Blake's Job, Kent's Hermit suffers without understanding why, yet ultimately attains spiritual transformation.

For all the equilibrium suggested by these images, Kent remained torn between Hildegarde and Kathleen. In Alaska he had implored Hildegarde to join him, but on Fox Island he realized his enduring love for Kathleen. She agreed to reconciliation only after he assured her he had ended the affair and would abandon his earlier troubling behavior, pointedly noting that other men had shown her attention.

Kent, in turn, claimed that his happiness was marred only by what Kathleen revealed in her letters: she refused his pleas to visit, making it "increasingly evident that but to save our marriage and support the family I must quit Alaska and go home."[82] In reality, by late 1918 he was plagued by jealous nightmares: "I woke up last night in bed shouting... Write to me and dispel, with your promises, carefully and fully made, all fear." His suspicions verged on the violent: "I think for jealousy I could kill a man. No—for jealously I could kill him myself."[83]

In November 1918, Kathleen learned, when visiting New York City, that while she had been living in near-poverty on Monhegan, Kent had lavished expensive jewelry on Hildegarde and paid her the equivalent of her Ziegfeld Follies salary to keep her from returning to the stage. As described above, Kathleen's indignation prompted Kent to break with Hildegarde that December. Kathleen, despite their turbulent marriage, remained the steadier partner.

On Christmas Day, Kent wrote Kathleen:

> Ah—I want you sweet wife. This day has been your day with us. I wanted, just before I lighted the candles, to sit down and write you the loving that was in my heart... Sweet mother, now as I write you and all the children have long been fast asleep ... it's next morning with you. I have believed today that I have been just as much in your thoughts as you have been in mine. I have thought that you missed me ever so much. And now I believe you to be dreaming of me as close beside you as your pillow.[84]

Two months later in February 1919 he reassured her he was "returning ... It will be somewhat hard to explain this to our friends and I must ask you to let me tell them the true cause ... that you are in so despondent mood

... that I must return home."⁸⁵ The truth was that it was Kent who was in a "despondent mood." As husband, Kent depended on Kathleen's willingness to remain; as artist, he relied on having a woman close at hand. In Alaska, amid psychic turmoil, he recognized that Kathleen—not Hildegarde—was his best option.

To Zigrosser he confessed: "I bitterly regret leaving that wonderful free spot—and just as the fairer weather approaches and I begin to see the true wonderland that surrounds this bay... Oh God, how beautiful these wild mountains are with the virgin sun upon them."⁸⁶ This bittersweet departure was accompanied with a sense of renewal:

> Fox Island will soon become in our memories like a dream or vision, a remote experience too wonderful, for the full liberty we knew there and the deep peace, to be remembered or believed in as a real experience in life. It was for us life as it should be, serene and wholesome; love—but no hate, faith without disillusionment, the absolute for the toiling hands of man and his soaring spirit—like Paradise.⁸⁷

CHAPTER 9

# Gentleman Farmer (1919–1922)

In Alaska, while struggling with the future of his marriage, Kent was also planning the next phase of his career. Often distracted by romantic entanglements, he was clear-headed in planning his professional advancement. In November, he told Zigrosser that he despised peddling his drawings to magazines and advertising firms: "I've been turning my own future prospects over ... I everlastingly dread the thought of having to begin the dreadful ordeal of the editors again ... I already begin to see myself as a rather ridiculous figure running here and there with my portfolio of ideas that nobody wants."

Instead of returning to Manhattan, "I figure that I could retire to the country ... and live possibly within $1500 a year. Of that sum I now get five hundred from my mother. The remaining thousand I want to raise." Kent believed himself an indefatigable worker who could possibly earn as much as ten thousand dollars a year. Yet he felt like "a valuable productive machine [who] cannot operate for lack of fuel." To remedy this, he proposed securing capital, "incorporate if necessary and issue bonds to cover one, two or three years, coupons redeemable yearly with interest added." He asked Zigrosser to make inquiries on his behalf.[88]

On a more personal note, Alaska had reinforced his desire to escape the city entirely: "It's a treat nowadays to live uninhabited. I am determined ... to get out of the city." He dreamed of moving with his family to a remote rural spot in New England.[89]

Kent was penniless. Kathleen had borrowed a thousand dollars to support herself and her three daughters. Still, there was good news: a collector had purchased a painting. Marie Sterner responded enthusiastically to the Alaska

## CHAPTER 9

drawings and was eager to show them at Knoedler. The exhibition opened less than a month after Kent's return. Most of the drawings sold within a week, The artist's indebtedness to Nietzsche and Blake was noted by many critics. *The New York Star*'s writer asserted: he has "gone out alone at night to interrogate the heavens." That write also observed: "tragedy is not yet his style ... And in spite of his own words, it has been decidedly larkish."[90]

Since Kent had agreed to having some of the drawings engraved and so, while the exhibit was still running, a few pieces were periodically removed from the exhibition and sent to an engraver. This led Kent to wonder if the prints could be assembled into a limited-edition book. The idea gained momentum when Kent reconnected with an old friend, George Putnam, who had returned from Oregon to join his family's publishing firm, G. P. Putnam's Sons. Specializing in adventure stories, Putnam realized a book about Kent's time in Alaska would be a natural fit for his list, especially when he learned that Kent had kept a journal while in Alaska—the contents of that diary had been sent as various intervals to Kathleen, who had shared them with family and friends. Putnam convinced Kent to combine the drawings and writings into a regular trade book.

Buoyed by the sale of the painting, the success of the Knoedler exhibition, and money from his mother, Kent decided in late May/early June to explore the Green Mountains in southwestern Vermont. He and Kathleen boarded a train in New York City, arrived at Bennington, then traveled north by train until they reached Arlington, 15 miles north of Bennington. Pleased by what they saw, they left the train. There, they discovered that John Fisher, a classmate of Kent's at Columbia, and his wife, the best-selling writer, Dorothy Canfield, lived nearby. The couple welcomed the Kents, insisted they stay with them and, as Kent recalled, "determined that we should settle thereabouts."[91]

Canfield, who had turned Arlington into a lively cultural center, was eager to add Kent to that community. She joined the Kents in their search for a home. Before long they found "Egypt," a hill farm in the northeast corner of Arlington on the slope of Red Mountain. The property—house and barn set in a hollow with spectacular views—was in disrepair. At $2,300, it was $1,300 over the Kents' budget. When Canfield immediately offered to lend them the difference, the Kents bought it.

## GENTLEMAN FARMER (1919–1922)

Kent immediately began making "Egypt" livable, while Canfield arranged for Kathleen and the children to stay in an old family house in the center of Arlington. Kent converted the interior of the dilapidated farmhouse by adding sleek modern lines. While working on the Alaska paintings, he used a barn adjacent to the house. To capture the best views on his property, he built a 12 by 15 foot shack near a bluff, a ten-minute walk from the house and barn. Two vantage points from the new studio can be seen in the Vermont paintings: one looking directly north, the other south.

"Egypt" was eight miles from the center of Arlington. Kent eventually obtained a driver's license and an automobile that made the commute—some of it through rough uphill terrain—less difficult. The local school was a three-mile round trip. During their first year at "Egypt,' the children walked there. However, Kathleen and the children spent the next three school years in Greenwich, Connecticut, where the children attended the progressive Englewood School. The couple's fifth child, Gordon, was born on October 1, 1920.

By the time the renovations were completed, the Kents were again strapped financially. Assistance was provided when George Putnam, a trained lawyer, offered assistance after learning of the financial scheme Kent had devised in Alaska. He advised Kent to incorporate himself. The resulting Corporation had four shareholders with an initial investment of $4,000 at $100 a share. Kent became general manager, was paid a salary in monthly installments of $155.66. Concerned that this venture might be seen in a negative light, Kent created a light-hearted stock certificate showing an apple tree, a snake slithering up its trunk and a disheartened Adam lying on the ground.

Incorporation provided Kent with much-needed financial backing. To that coup was added the tremendous success of the exhibition of Alaska paintings at Knoedler in March 1920. That same month, *Wilderness*, with a preface by Canfield, became a runaway best-seller. *The New Statesman* lavished warm praise on it and claimed it was the best American book since Whitman's *Leaves of Grass*. When Sterner left Knoedler in 1921, Kent helped her organize the Junior Art Patrons of Art exhibition, a survey of the history of American art. Seven of his canvases were included. Three days before the opening, two sold for $2,500 and $3,500.

## CHAPTER 9

Suddenly famous, Kent moved quickly to promote himself and safeguard his reputation. Zigrosser recalled: "He often went out with black tie and dinner coat, and moved in the New York or the Long Island estates of the Pulitzers and the Whitneys."[92] He often spent weekends at the Manhasset home of Frederika Vanderbilt and Ralph Pulitzer and—occasionally—visited his wife and children in Greenwich.

Despite his cultivation of wealthy patrons, Kent reflected on his artistic goals. "I want tranquility and it must be through absolute precision of line and color and the elimination of every unessential thing until the very breaking point is at hand—and there stop."[93] He confronted himself point blank:

> In my work I seem to have begun all over again. I'm not discouraged by it for I've been working hard upon problems that I want to master; studying, really, as if I were a beginner. I suppose the harvest will come sometime ... Out of this study I hope to evolve a form of simple characterization. It goes against my nature to work without possessing a thorough and exact knowledge of it. Out of this one can evolve ... that simple statement which is his art.[94]

In Alaska, he had already achieved "absolute perfection of line and the elimination of every unessential thing." In Vermont in 1920, he sought to add a "form of simple characterization." Reconciling those goals was not easy. He may have wondered if the Vermont paintings needed "characterization"—a narrative element he had avoided in his Alaska work.

A bird of prey swoops down to catch a squirrel while a spikehorn buck looks on in *Shadows of Evening* (1921–1923). In *The Trapper* (1921), a hunter carries both his catch and the trap that snared it. Without the hunter and his dog, that composition—with its deep snow, intersecting shadows, half-moon, hills, and sky—resembles the Alaska paintings.

By adding storylines to these new works, Kent returned in part to his Newfoundland practice of inserting symbols into landscapes. *Autumn* (1923–1927) recalls that approach. The androgynous figure at its center, set against the dramatic Valley of Vermont, could be either in despair or exultation. The uncertainty about its gender and emotion may mirror Kent's own state of mind in "Egypt." Was he renewed, or still unsure about the direction of his art and life? In Alaska's isolation, he believed he had found a way forward. In Vermont, that conviction gradually faded.

GENTLEMAN FARMER (1919–1922)

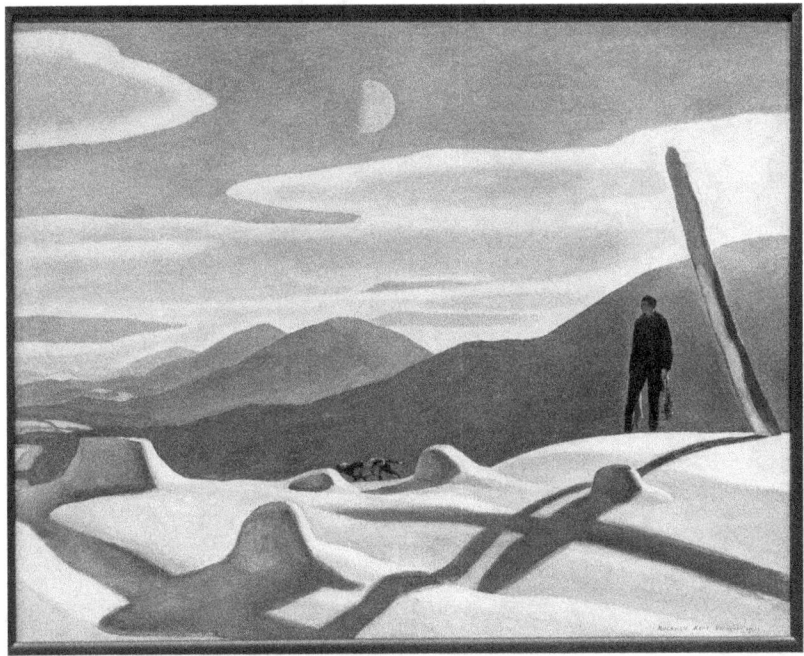

**Figure 18:** *The Trapper.* 1921. Oil on canvas. 86 × 112 cm. Whitney Museum of American Art.

## CHAPTER 10

# Lover (1922–1928)

> *Wild* oats ... can last ... for years. And the soil of America and of New York in particular, the temperature and humidity of New York in the post-war decade, would prove ideal for their germination. Not that I *sowed* the oats; carried about with me they just slipped out. And the crop, threatening to overwhelm me with its luxuriousness, was soon to drive me, all but literally hell bent, to that far southern Land of Fire, Tierra del Fuego.[95]

Kent's playful tone in the above passage conceals more than it reveals. Although Kent could be a loving, often indulgent parent, family life bored him. The resulting weariness sometimes boiled over into anger toward the children. He had reconciled with Kathleen, but fidelity was beyond him—especially when he was able to spend considerable amounts of time alone in New York. The children, meanwhile, witnessed frequent bickering between their father and mother.

Visits to New York were prompted by a new project. In addition to working on his Vermont landscapes, he collaborated with George Chappell on dozens of illustrated stories for the *New York Tribune*—a form of work about which, as mentioned above, he had serious reservations.

Once again, Kent could not settle down to the semblance of a stable regime. He may have felt he should, but he simply could not. In mythological terms, he saw himself as a twentieth-century Odysseus—although Odysseus had returned to Penelope and Ithaca. His landscapes of Maine, Newfoundland and Alaska had been forged in settings he regarded as raw and untamed, painted in near-total isolation. Vermont was different. Its gentler scenery could be observed from the family home. Although he created some outstanding landscapes in Vermont, a restlessness for harsher, more demanding terrain gnawed at him. He was poignantly reminded of his time in Alaska when Lars Olson stayed with him briefly at "Egypt."

Kent worked best when the wilderness outside matched the wilderness within—the psychic landscapes he was instinctively drawn to. That was the kind of stimulation he knew (perhaps unconsciously) that allowed him to unleash his creativity. His landscape paintings capture moments of stillness in which he was able to access the center of himself—that portion of his psyche that cherished tranquility in remote, primordial locations.

Zigrosser, worried that Kent spent too much of his time, cultivating the rich and powerful, warned him: "I can't help feeling that when you are in the city you waste your superb energy on unessential things."[96]

In 1922, Kent was fleeing from Lydia, a "witch" who had lured him and another man into an "enchanted wood." They reached a pond, whereupon the lady announced, "whichever of you swims across to meet me on the other side, I will be his." Kent plunged in, reached her first—and then learned—"as the years would prove, [she] had only wet her shoes."[97] In recounting this incident, Kent describes it in language reminiscent of a Grimm Brothers fairytale. What he may be implying is that he was bested in the competition for her affections.

Kent resolved: "If there's a worse place in the world than New York City, I will go there." Remote Tierra del Fuego was hardly the "worse place in the world" but one Kent knew would test him severely.[98] George Putnam, who knew something of dangerous expeditions—he was married to Amelia Earhart—advised his friend to consult Colonel Charles Wellington Furlong, who had served in Tierra del Fuego in 1907–1909. Furlong warned Kent how dangerous his itinerary could be: "Southern Patagonia has been in the throes the last six months because of desperate bands of outlaws burning ranch houses and committing all kinds of depredations." He added: "it would be unwise if not unsafe to go into that part of the country right now."[99] Kent was not a man to be dissuaded by caution.

Furlong insisted Kent take a gun: "If you meet a stranger and, he, let's say, asks you for the time of day, be agreeable, tell him the time—*but have your gun ready at the trigger.*" Although he considered himself a pacifist, Kent prudently purchased a long-barreled Colt .22 caliber revolver.[100]

Tierra del Fuego is an archipelago at the southernmost tip of South America; its southernmost headland, Cape Horn, is infamous for violent seas where the Atlantic and Pacific converge. The waters are treacherous, whipped by fierce winds and deadly currents. Kent was traveling to a place just above Antarctica—before he had explored Alaska, which is just below the Arctic. In journeying to Tierra del Fuego, Kent was searching for a comparable backwoods.

In Alaska, he had lived in the bush. In South America, he wanted to explore a similar rugged landscape, but he was also determined to sail around Cape Horn to duplicate the accomplishment of Richard Henry Dana, Jr., the New England born explorer and the author of *Two Years Before the Mast*.

In late May 1922, Kathleen and Zigrosser accompanied Kent to the Grace Line pier in Brooklyn, where he departed aboard the steamer *Curaca* on a six-week voyage through the Strait of Magellan. Aboard ship, Kent resorted to his penchant for practical jokes. This time he focused on "Sparks," the young, gangly radio operator. This fellow suddenly received letters from an unknown sweetheart; firecrackers were thrown into his cabin; when he experienced stomach pains (probably from food poisoning) the ship's doctor informed him he was pregnant.

Kent signed on as the ship's assistant freight clerk, which gave him plenty of free time. He formed a bond with Ole Ytterock, the third mate. The two hatched a plan that upon arrival at Punta Arenas in Chile, they would purchase a large lifeboat and equip her. The first hurdle was to find and outfit a vessel. Kent bought a 26-foot lifeboat off a wrecked freighter for $20, then spent two months to refit it as a cruising sailboat named *Kathleen*. On her very first day out sailing, the boat proved to be alarmingly leaky and almost sank.

Another three weeks were spent making the vessel sound. Finally, Kent and Ytterock set forth down Admiralty Sound. Without an engine, *Kathleen* was powerless against strong westerlies. At that point, Kent and Ytterock anchored the boat in a cove, hiked south on the mountainous portion of Tierra del Fuego and arrived at Ushuaia on Beagle Channel, where they chartered another boat, *Kathleen II*. That vessel was just as hapless as her predecessor. Though the new boat got close enough to see Cape Horn, Kent was forced to turn back. After this incident, Kent made arrangements to leave. He sold *Kathleen II*, set off hiking across eastern Tierra del Fuego,

CHAPTER 10

was picked up by a driver with a Model-T Ford, and eventually arrived at Punta Arenas to board the *S.S. Toluma* home.

Although much of Kent's energy in Tierra del Fuego had been expended on the doomed Cape Horn project, he spent a considerable amount of his time on land hiking, drawing and painting. When he arrived back in Vermont in the winter of 1923, he had an abundance of work to complete. He had promised Putnam the book that became *Voyaging: Southward from the Strait of Magellan* (1924).

That narrative and its illustrations do not contain the range of intimate reflections and piercing imagery of *Wilderness*. The text is largely a travel log of Kent's adventures on the two small ships he piloted in quest of Cape Horn; he provided well-turned observations on the locales he visited; the illustrations document the places described in prose. The book was published to great acclaim. *The New Republic* rhapsodized, "the land lives. A land where roses are as big as sun-flowers, where gales gnaw against bleak cliffs " *The Nation* claimed that Kent caught "the wild beauty of this ominous region—iron crags ringed with the froth of blown surf, wind-tortured trees, distant peaks incrusted with dazzling snow; but out of the very heart of this bewildering beauty emanates a sense of unseen presences appallingly, implacably hostile to man."

The landscape paintings from Tierra del Fuego are powerful in markedly different ways from those done in Alaska. As in *Admiralty Sound, Tierra del Fuego* (c. 1922–1925), muted tones of gray, brown, and blues capture the desolate terrain of this lonely part of the world. Its melancholy stillness is powerfully rendered. These new landscapes show a place "vast, untrodden and but little navigated wilderness." Kent perceived it as comparable to Alaska "in its grandeur. [But this] whole region is surpassing it in the infinite variety of its forms, and imbued with that special glamour which the human soul finds in the utterly unknown."[101] The Tierra del Fuego canvases are more stylized than the Alaskan ones and do not possess their rugged grandeur.

The outward calm of the summer of 1923 masked private tensions. On the surface, it was a joyous one for the Kent family in Vermont. Beneath the façade, however, was Kent's decision that his family should travel to Europe that November—he would join them later. Kathleen may have seen this as

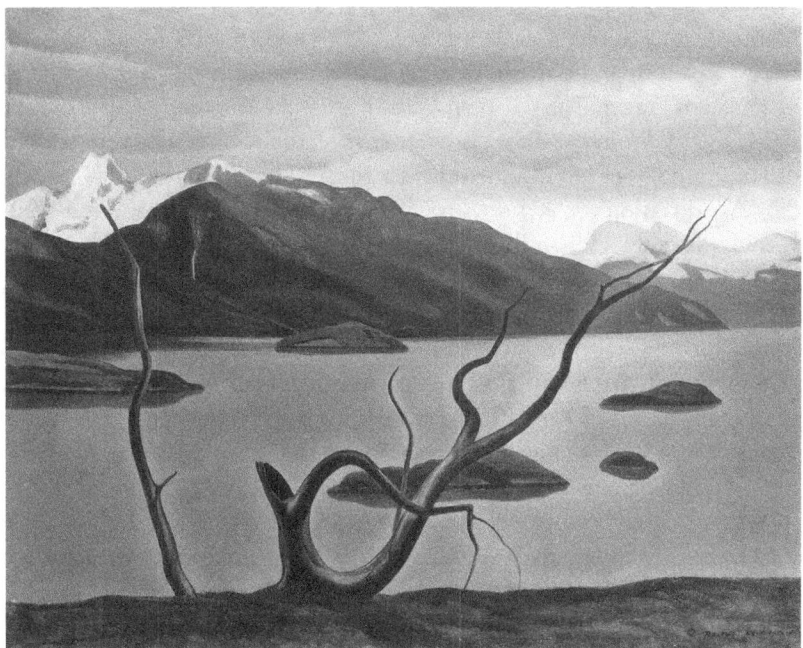

**Figure 19:** *Admiralty Sound, Tierra del Fuego.* 1925. 86 × 111 cm. Oil on canvas. Heritage Museum, Saint Petersburg.

a ploy to remove her and the children so that he could pursue yet another affair. Nevertheless, she and the children left on schedule in November 1923. Kathleen was right to be suspicious. After she departed, Kent hired Maureen—like Hildegarde a show-girl whom he had employed as a model—to type the manuscript of *Voyaging*. She was, as Kent recalled, a "dark-haired, grey-eyed, Celtic type that is so beautiful."

While Kathleen and the children were in Europe, Kent met F. DeWitt Wells, a retired Justice in the municipal court of New York and a Putnam author. At the age of 49, Wells wanted to fulfill a childhood fantasy of sailing a small boat from Denmark to the United States following the same course Leif Ericson had taken in 1000 AD. Wells lacked the experience in pursuing his dream and so asked for the artist's advice. Wells finally decided to purchase an appropriate vessel on which he wanted experienced sailors to accompany him. Kent was his first choice.

## CHAPTER 10

An aficionado of the Icelandic sagas, this was an offer Kent could not refuse. In addition, he would have the chance to visit his wife and children in southern France. The two men sailed from New York on the S.S. *Homeric* in May 1924. From the outset of their voyage, the two men bickered. Wells did not mind Kent talking about his sex life, but he disapproved of his companion's flirtatious behavior with female passengers. Kent suspected Wells was homosexual and, on those grounds, disapproved of him.

Wells was contemptuous of what he considered Kent's anti-intellectualism: "He does not care to see anything in Europe... but would look at the ceiling of the Sistine Chapel, visit the grave of Goethe...[for him] History [is] repetitious & only the mountains, the sea, uninhabited regions and icebergs are significant."[102] In Paris, Kent decided not to join Wells in Copenhagen and visited his family in France. But soon a telegram arrived from Wells beseeching help.

When Kent arrived, Wells had managed to hire the ship's original crew plus some others to man the double-ended Colin Archer-style cutter called *Shanghai* he had purchased. Kent decided he was not needed and, for the second time, abandoned the project. On what proved a perilous journey, the ship got caught in a hurricane and struck a huge rock on Møns Klint in southeastern Denmark. No one perished, but the cutter was destroyed.

Kent borrowed money from Zigrosser to return home. Later, Rocky, who had been offered a scholarship at a private school in the Berkshires, traveled back alone to the States on a Fabre liner—Kathleen and the other children remained back in France. Expecting to meet his son in New York, Kent journeyed from Vermont to the Brooklyn Docks to meet him. He was aghast when the boy was not there. He later learned that the ship's steward, contrary to what had been agreed, had insisted the boy disembark at New London, Connecticut, the ship's first port of call. Penniless and confused, Rocky was given money by Travelers Aid and eventually wound up at Auntie Jo's in Tarrytown. Outraged, Kent sued. He even blocked one of the company's ships, filled with passengers, from sailing. The newspapers reveled in this debacle.

Although Kent's anger was justifiable, the incident, perhaps at an unconscious level, triggered suppressed feelings about how as a child his father had been precipitously snatched away from him. He might have seen Rocky's plight as a reflection of his own early loss.

Kent had come to the realization that his marriage had reached breaking point. "And when Kathleen, facing up to reality, wrote suggesting a divorce whenever either of us, with a second marriage in mind, might ask for it, I—far too readily it seems to me in retrospect—accepted it. I held myself from then on to be free."[103] When Kent did find a woman he wanted to marry, he and Kathleen divorced in September 1925.

However, the lady in question, Kent claimed, fell in love with someone else. This was not true. In fact, Kent's description of this new person suggests that he was not infatuated.

> She wasn't beautiful; she was, in fact, quite plain. Yet she was attractive, strangely, by virtue of the quaint and utterly irrational mind and wayward temperament that characterized her as a problem child; attractive and through the indulgence of her moods and prejudices to which she was accustomed, at times infuriating.[104]

Their relationship was sometimes acerbic. When the lady told him that one of her arms had been paralyzed from childhood, Kent boasted he could cure her ailment. "I swung my arm and slapped her face, just once. Then I sat down. She was already up and raining blows on me."

After relating this incident Kent added: "'That blow,' her psychiatrist told me later, 'was a stroke of genius. She'll never have that trouble again.'" He asked Kent: "why don't you take charge of her? You can do more with her than I can. Take charge of her? Darn it, I did. Accordingly, I wrote to Kathleen. And in June, bidding my problem bride-to-be a very fond farewell, I sailed for France."[105]

This mystery woman was not the writer, artist and traveler Ernesta Drinker, who was ten years younger than Kent and with whom he was also having an affair at about this time. In 1923, she had divorced her first husband, William C. Bullitt. Unlike his previous lovers, Ernesta was cosmopolitan, sophisticated and well educated. Her family was an elite one in Philadelphia—her father had been president of Lehigh University in nearby Bethlehem. Kent wrote to her at the height of their affair:

> Sweetheart, I cannot write. For nearly two hours I have sat here, abandoned to my thoughts of you. I am drunk with the memory of you—and the hope. "Ernesta," "Ernesta!" I cry, as if my cry for you might bring you to me; and you, dear heart, dear sweet, sweet love of mine, are of my hands, my lips, my eyes, of every sense awakened into consciousness, and of my ardent spirit, the whole and last desire. Dear girl—I am enveloped by your loveliness.[106]

## CHAPTER 10

Ernesta refused to commit herself to Kent; in fact, she was hesitant to tell him she loved him. In response, he told her a story about a heart, never given away, that deserted its owner. Ernesta, probably offended, replied that she would not marry him. Kent was furious. The relationship ended abruptly.

Shortly afterwards, in Antibes, Kent pursued Marya Mannes, the daughter of a friend, but she, like Ernesta, found his intensity overpowering. He was determined to fall in love again. Back in the States, he met Frances Lee Higgins, a 26 old divorcee with a young son, who had recently moved to New York from Virginia. She quickly became the new dream woman. Kent claimed to be enthralled from the first moment he met her at a luncheon party at Manhasset: "I had no ideas; no ears; no thoughts, for any other. ... I read her candor in her countenance, and I felt the warmth and goodness of her heart. I loved her without doubt, or caution, or reserve."[107] They married in New York City on April 15, 1926.

When he fell in love, Kent declared his passionate feelings forcefully. That approach did not work with Ernesta or Marya. Those two women may have sensed that his ardor might subside as quickly as it had arisen. Such assumptions would have been accurate, although Kent apparently never realized this. At the outset of an affair, he could not envision that he would tire of the love object.

In his amorous relationships, Kent placed women on pedestals. But sooner or later, they were dislodged. It could be argued that Kent was an incurable romantic always on the lookout for a new adventure. That might be true, but he most certainly saw women as secondary to men and as entities who could be bent to his will. In addition, Kent was never really secretive about his affairs—he took pleasure in broadcasting them. In that sense, he was an exhibitionist.

Kent valued solitude. Most of his paintings were done on expeditions—away from the company of women. He often wanted to be alone, but he also wanted frequent sexual encounters. There was a wide discrepancy between these two states of existence. He never found a way to resolve such conflicted emotions.

He also felt that he had the right to pursue any entanglement he chose, even though such an imbroglio violated commitments he had made. In a sense, he thought artists were a special breed who enjoyed special prerogatives that allowed them to disregard societal norms. When he found his "Self"—and disregarded his "Better Self"—he thought he found his métier.

Kent and Frances honeymooned in the Adirondacks and then traveled to northwest Ireland, where Kent painted. Kent's status as an artist rose steadily in the Twenties. In April 1924 he showed his Tierra del Fuego drawings at the Weyhe Gallery; the Wildenstein Galleries gave him his first retrospective the same month; the watercolors he did in southern France were exhibited at the Weyhe Gallery in February 1926; the Irish watercolors and drawings were at the Weyhe in March 1927; some Irish and other works could be seen at Wildenstein in April 1927.

In the autumn of 1926, Kent and Frances moved to 3 Washington Square South, but Kent was not at ease in New York City which he labeled "The Gold Camp," a euphemism for the array of young women there and the other, various temptations that the metropolis offered. He needed to find a semblance of quietude. In the summer of 1927 the couple moved to Woodstock, New York. (As part of the divorce settlement, Kathreen obtained "Egypt"). The following summer they purchased an Adirondack farmstead.

> Near, but not in view of, the village of Au Sable Forks [New York] ... lay an exceptionally level hundred acre place of clear and cultivated land, a farm, the view from there, the view of Whiteface Mountain in the west and, southwards, of the major Adirondack peaks and ranges, surpassed belief. It took but one look from the country road that bounded it to capture me.[108]

He called his new home Asgaard. In Norse mythology, Asgaard is the heavenly dwelling of the gods. Kent felt he had discovered a new home similar to "Egypt" but one imbued with even greater restorative powers.

This time, Kent did not build the new house, but he drew up the plans that R. Prescott and Sons of nearby Keeseville constructed within four months. The house was set in a grove of pines facing the mountain view to the west. The living room and eight bedrooms faced west; his studio faced north; the kitchen and dinner alcove faced east, as did the five bathrooms. The house was finished in white clapboard and trim. Bright, intense colors on the woodwork and built-in furniture were prominent in the interior that had plenty of space to display examples of Kent's art and memorabilia he had collected on his travels.

## CHAPTER 10

For him, the "test of a good house is how good a time people can have in it."[109] His new home also reflected the financial success he had finally achieved. It had a well-stocked open bar, a tennis court, and a swimming pool. Horses and Great Danes wandered the grounds. One friend recalled that the guests included "eminent publishers, actresses, members of the Vermont Symphony Orchestra, ... local contractors, assorted artists and near-by roadhouse keepers." These guests entertained "each other with acrobatics on the lawn, high diving, ground and lofty tumbling, quartet playing, and kayak stunting."[110] Despite the frantic lifestyle at Asgaard, Kent rose every morning at five, sometimes swam and then retreated to his studio for a full day's work.

Soon after Asgaard was finished, a friend mentioned to Kent that his son was sailing to Greenland in a small boat. "God! May I go with him?," the artist eagerly responded. "And so it came about that when on June 17th [1929]—less than a year later—the cutter *Direction* set out from Baddeck, Nova Scotia, for Greenland, of the three men who manned her I was one."[111] When Kent set off on this new adventure, he was in the midst of many commitments, especially book illustrations—an essential element in his livelihood.

CHAPTER 11

# Illustrator (1925–1949)

In a fine touch of irony, in the midst of his affair with Ernesta Drinker, Kent was illustrating a 12 volume edition of *The Memoirs of Jacques Casanova de Seingalt* (1925). While in Europe in the summer of 1924, he was asked to smuggle Arthur Machen's translation of this notorious work into the United States. He agreed but wondered how he could get them across the border. To his relief, that scheme was abandoned and in its place a "bona-fide American edition" was commissioned.

"These ... were to be my first venture—beyond the illustrating of my own books and the far earlier *Architec-tonics*—into a field of work that from then on in and for years to come was to be the mainstay of the family's support."[112] This was an enormous undertaking—"any one volume of the twelve held enough inspiration to have elsewhere halted further reading."[113] Although he did not state so, Kent must have identified with the sexual escapades of Casanova.

Following this enormous project, Bennett Cerf and Donald Klopfer asked him in 1928 to design the logo for their new imprint, Random House, and to illustrate their first book, a translation of Voltaire's *Candide*, as both a trade book and a hand-colored limited edition. Since Kent had already immersed himself in eighteenth-century customs and dress for the *Casanova*, he was happy to apply his research to this commission.

By then, his livelihood came not only from his oils, watercolors, and drawings but also from a wide assortment of commercial projects, especially newspaper and magazine advertisements. From 1928 onwards, a significant portion of his earnings came from book illustration. His commissions included Thornton Wilder's *The Bridge of San Luis Rey* (1929), Pushkin's *The Gabrieliad* (1929), Melville's *Moby Dick* (1930), Chaucer's *Canterbury*

*Tales* (1930), Shakespeare's *Venus and Adonis* (1931), *Beowulf* (1932), Samuel Butler's *Erewhon* (1934), the plays of Shakespeare (1936), *The Saga of Gisli, Son of Sour* (1936), Whitman's *Leaves of Grass* (1936), Esther Shephard's *Paul Bunyan* (1941), Goethe's *Faust* (1941), and Boccaccio's *The Decameron* (1949). Alongside his landscape paintings, drawings and wood engravings, Kent's book illustrations stand among his greatest achievements.

Illustrating Chaucer and Shakespeare allowed Kent to create vividly drawn characters. *The Decameron*, like *Casanova*, revels in amorous pursuits. *The Saga of Gisli* unfolds in thirteenth-century Iceland, another northern land close to his heart. The temptation to overreach is central to *Faust*. These narratives echoed themes that resonated deeply with Kent. Yet three—*Moby Dick*, *Leaves of Grass* and *Paul Bunyan*—struck him deeply because each explored issues of his identity as an American.

The commission to illustrate *Moby Dick* was arranged with William Kittredge of Chicago's Lakeside Press in the autumn of 1926. Kittridge invited him to illustrate one of four American classics that were to be issued in limited editions as examples of Lakeside's craftsmanship in bookmaking. The fee to each illustrator was to be one thousand dollars; and the book proposed to Kent was Dana's *Two Years Before the Mast*. He liked that book; but he liked another book much more. That book was *Moby Dick*.[114] Earlier, Carl Zigrosser had approached Alfred Knopf about publishing such an edition with illustrations by Kent. Knopf was interested but his offer fell short of what the artist considered acceptable.

The Melville illustrations, done over almost four years, Kent recalled "proved a monumental task, not only in their actual making but in the preliminary research [including the Museum of Natural History in New York and the whaling museum in New Bedford, Massachusetts] but also upon which they were based."[115] The book was originally to be issued in one volume; when Kent asked for two, Kittridge not only agreed but doubled his payment; when the artist subsequently pleaded for three volumes, the publisher consented and generously raised his payment to $4,000.

*Moby Dick* contains 135 chapter plus an epilogue. The Kittridge edition [1,000 copies] contains 280 images by Kent [the Random House trade edition, 270]. In an astounding oversight, the dust jacket of the Random House edition omitted Melville's name. The publisher claimed: "We were so excited about [the book], we forgot to put Herman Melville's name on the cover, so our edition of *Moby Dick*, to the vast amusement of everybody, said only *Moby Dick*, illustrated by Rockwell Kent"[116] *Vanity Fair* pounced: "Of 1930 the literary event/ Was the Random House edition of Moby Kent."[117] In both editions, the 1851 publication date is evoked through illustrations designed to resemble wood engravings, reinforcing the novel's nineteenth-century origins. The wealth of imagery does not swamp the text; instead, it makes the book feel almost co-authored by Melville and Kent. In preparing his illustrations, Kent freely borrowed from earlier depictions of whales and even re-used some of his own images from *Wilderness*. His identification with the voyage of the *Pequod* was a complete one. The sea—its power and turbulence—had always been central to his own self-discovery.

At its heart, *Moby Dick* is a revenge tale framed in symbolic terms. Ahab's quest to kill the whale that took his leg can be read as a bid to reclaim his eviscerated masculinity—or, more broadly, as man's doomed attempt to bend nature to his will. In that sense, the novel holds an ecological undertone. It can also be read as a parable encapsulating the clash between the life force represented by the white whale and the death drive embodied in Ahab. Kent's illustrations mirror this cosmic struggle. His whale studies are majestic, and his translucent white *Moby Dick* unforgettable. Ishmael, the lone survivor, appears as a sincere youth; other characters verge on caricature. Father Mapp is a man of tormented faith; Ahab, a malignant figure poised between light and shadow. Since Melville's prose charts the tension between humanity and the grandeur of nature, Kent provided its ideal visual counterpart.

William Kittridge was also the printer of the 1936 Heritage Press edition of *Leaves of Grass*, Whitman's elegant spiritual autobiography in verse that celebrates the immanence of a spiritual force governing existence. On hearing of Kent's involvement, Kitteridge exclaimed: "We consider it an act of God that Rockwell Kent is going to illustrate Walt Whitman's *Leaves of Grass*. The greatest American illustrator and the greatest American poet! What an association! The book should be a sensation and one of the finest American books of all time."[118]

If *Moby Dick* depicts man's war with nature, *Leaves of Grass* exalts man's harmony with it. Kent's pen and ink drawings employ a wide range of symbols to enrich Whitman's reflections. There is but one full-page illustration—a frontispiece showing a naked man floating upwards in transcendence. Flanking him are green lines and, at the far left stars blaze in the night sky. Here, man is rendered as an integral part of the vast transcendent natural order.

## CHAPTER 11

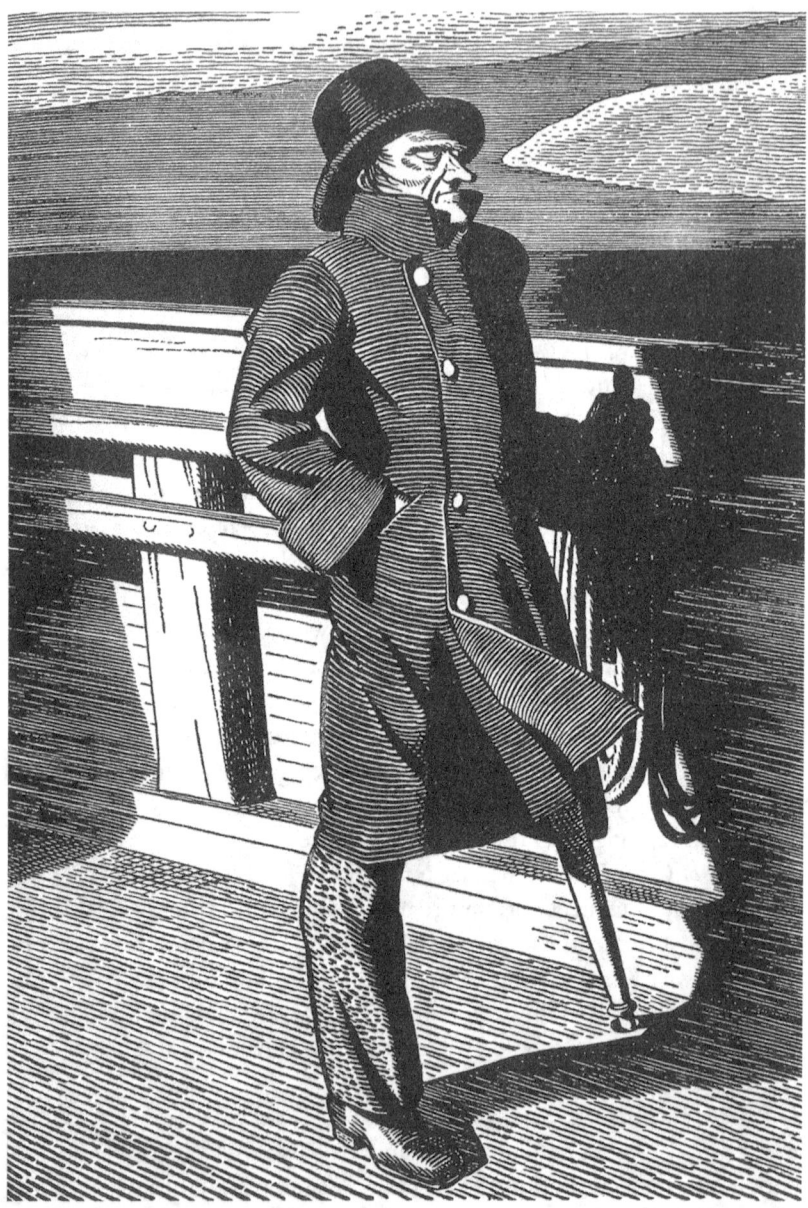

**Figure 20:** Ahab. *Moby Dick*. 1930.

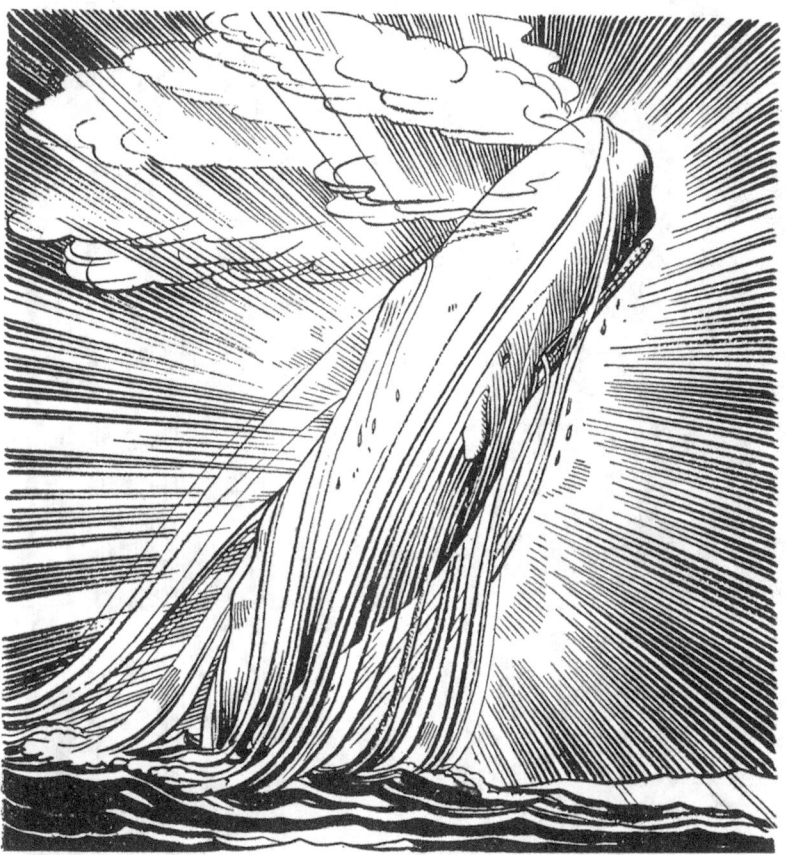

**Figure 21:** Moby Dick. *Moby Dick*. 1930.

## CHAPTER 11

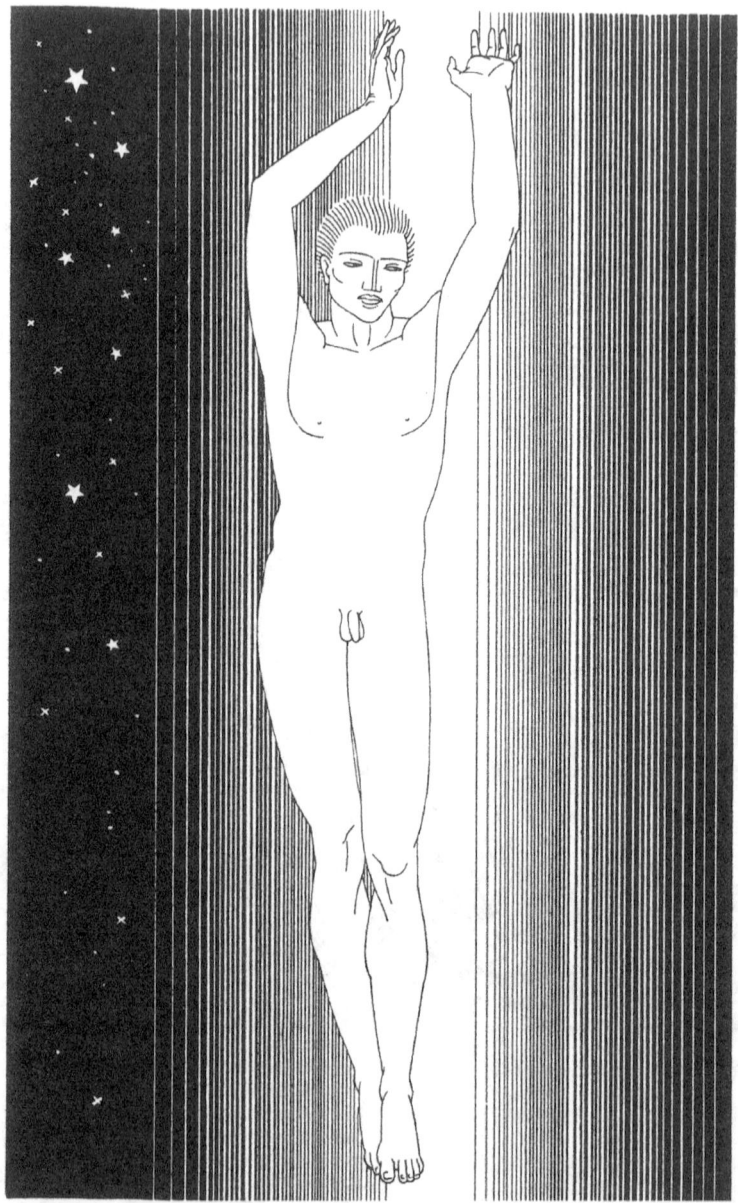

**Figure 22:** Frontispiece. *Leaves of Grass*. 1936.

The legend of Paul Bunyan, rooted in the lumber camps of the United States and Canada, first appeared in print in the *Duluth News Tribune* in 1904:

> His pet joke and the one with which the green horn at the camp is sure to be tried, consists of a series of imaginative tales about the year Paul Bunyan lumbered in North Dakota. The great Paul is represented as getting out countless millions of timber in the year of the "blue snow." The men's shanty in his camp covered a half section and the mess camp was a stupendous affair. The range on which an army of cooks prepared the beans and "red horse" was so long that when the cook wanted to grease it up for the purpose of baking the wheat cakes in the morning, they strapped two large hams to his feet and started him running up and down a half mile of black glistening stove top.[119]

The exploits of this gigantic figure draw heavily on ancient heroic traditions, especially the labors of Hercules. For Kent—who in Maine and Alaska had felled trees and cleared virgin forest—Paul Bunyan's feats struck a chord. In *Wilderness*, Kent had depicted himself in the midst of such labors, and would have felt kinship with the larger-than-life heroism they implied.

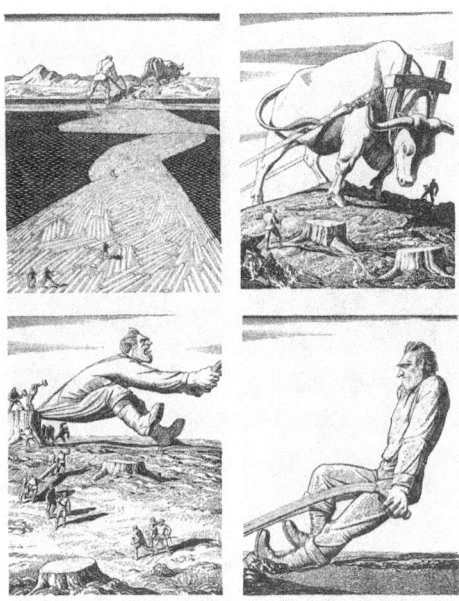

**Figure 23:** *Illustrations from Paul Bunyan.* 1941.

## CHAPTER 11

In each series of book illustrations, Kent sought to distill and illuminate the essence of the text. His *Moby Dick* images may be his most remarkable achievement in the genre. Melville and Whitman, together, present two visions of humanity's place in nature: in conflict and in accord. By spring 1928, Kent had moved to Asgaard and was still settling in. Even as he labored over *Moby Dick*, another northern landscape—Greenland—beckoned.

CHAPTER 12

# Explorer (1929–1932)

The prospect of visiting Greenland had long lingered in the back of Kent's mind: "From my first reading of the *Njal* saga twenty years before …through all that was recorded of the discovery and settlement of Greenland … how had I hoped to someday, somehow, see the hallowed lands of those heroic people."[120] Now, suddenly, a once of a lifetime opportunity presented itself—an invitation to explore a northern land that had long fueled his imagination. Kent instinctively knew that the chance to paint there was one he could not ignore.

Joining him on *Direction*—a sturdy thirty-three-feet adaptation of Colin Archer's redningskotte (Norwegian rescue boat)—were two twenty-year-old supposedly experienced sailors. The vessel had neither radio nor engine. In hindsight, Kent would wonder whether the boat was not as seaworthy as he had believed. That proved to be correct.

When he arrived in Baddeck, Nova Scotia, from where the voyage was to begin, Kent found the boat in disarray: among other issues, perishable goods had been left to rot. Nevertheless, the trio set sail under bright sunlight on June 17, 1929. Soon it became apparent that *Direction* would not beat windward, was over rigged and, in other ways, ill-suited to be the first yacht to sail from North America to Greenland.

They crossed the Cabot Strait and traveled up the west coast of Newfoundland where they narrowly avoided collision with a massive iceberg. After clearing the Strait of Belle Isle, they paused few days at Battle Harbor before setting off into open sea on July 5. On July 9, they sighted the coast of Greenland and headed toward Godthaab, the region's largest settlement. They anchored in a small fjord for the night, but the safe harbor proved to be a funnel for fierce winds. Within an hour, *Direction* sank on July 15.

## CHAPTER 12

Kent, who had considerably more experience in such catastrophes, set out alone to find Narsak, the closest settlement. After 36 hours, he reached there. From Narsak, Inuit kayakers, accompanied by Kent, set off for the wreck. When they arrived, they discovered that the two young men had done their best to salvage what they could from the vessel that was then towed to Godthaab.

Making the best of a bad situation, Kent remained in Greenland from July to September painting "constantly, for it was as a natural outpouring of my enthusiasm for all that I beheld in that vast wonderland of sea and mountains."[121] He later provided a blow-by-blow account of this perilous voyage in *N by E* (1930).

In September, Kent sailed from Godthaab to Copenhagen. He was astonished to discover that two of greatest of the Arctic explorers—Knud Rasmussen and Peter Freuchen—were on board. Kent formed friendships with them. Rasmussen invited him to stay with his family; Freuchen welcomed him to his island homestead, Enehøje. Both Danes encouraged Kent, when he could, to return to see more of Greenland.

Frances was waiting when the ship docked at Copenhagen. Accompanying her were unfinished *Moby Dick* drawings. Rasmussen presented Kent with a copy of his book *Across Arctic America: Narrative of the First Thule Expedition* (1927) that had been recently published by their mutual friend, George Putnam. In it, Rasmussen described racial and cultural similarities between the Indigenous of Alaska to those in Greenland. That connection fostered Kent's decision to return to Greenland.

Back at Asgaard, Kent had many pressing assignments, including work based on his Greenland material. So it was not until late spring 1931 that Kent and Frances returned to Copenhagen. From there, that June, they sailed on the steamer *Disco*. Frances stayed aboard until the ship reached the Faroe Islands. Kent went on alone. "My own short stay to Greenland in 1929," he recalled, "had filled me with a longing to return and spend a winter there, to see and experience the Far North at its spectacular 'worst'; to know the people and, and as far as could be, share their way of life."[122]

Freuchen has suggested Kent stay at Igdlorssuit, a small village on Ubekendt Island about 225 miles north of the Arctic Circle. There, Kent revived his carpentry skills by acquiring sufficient lumber to build a small, one room house. The villagers were impressed both by his craftsmanship and immense charm. Kent arranged for Salamina, a young widow with three children, to become his *kifak*, housekeeper. The Dames provided him with a small motorboat with which he could explore the coast.

"I sought out Salamina ... I found her to be a handsome, well-built woman of perhaps thirty, dark haired but as lightly complexioned as a swarthy European. She had great poise and dignity." Without stating so, Kent implied she did not look Inuit; he was hinting that she would make a suitable sexual companion. In response to his invitation, Salamina replied: "I will come. I'll stay with you a while. And if I like it, I'll stay always."[123] Salamina and Kent quickly became a couple and partied with many of the Inuit at Igdlorssuit. In addition to working arduously, Kent found that the dark nights in his new setting became "a period of the greatest social liveliness."[124]

In establishing a daily rhythm at Igdlorssuit, Kent sought not only artistic inspiration but also companionship—including sexual intimacy. Since he never kept such relationships from his partners, it is likely Frances knew of his involvement with Salamina. Although Salamina became jealous of Kent's flirtatious behavior with other women, she moved out of their small house in the summer of 1932 when Frances arrived in Greenland. Kent met his wife at Godhavn and returned with her to Igdlorssuit, where they stayed until September before departing for Copenhagen.

Two years later, in July 1934, Kent returned to Igdlorssuit—this time accompanied by his 13-year-old son, Gordon. There he painted and completed the text and illustrations for *Salamina*, an account of his 1931–1932 stay.

In *It's Me O Lord*, Kent reflected on bringing his son along. "That decision proved exactly right. It put him there with Greenland boys of his own age, on the threshold of manhood when boy stop *playing* hunters and become them in dead earnest."[125] Like Rocky in Alaska, Gordon adapted easily to the challenges of the Far North.

When *Salamina* was published, Louis Untermeyer penned a limerick on a greeting card he sent to Kent:

> A vigorous painter named KENT
> Said, "I figure my time is well spent
> In rubbing the noses
> Of She-Esquimauxes
> To further my evil intent."

CHAPTER 12

Frances had been planning to join her husband in Greenland but chose the warmer climate of Arizona. When Kent and Gordon left Greenland for Europe that summer, he received a telegram informing him that his wife and her son had been badly injured in a car accident in Tucson. By the time Kent reached her side, she was well on the way in recovering from major surgery.

In Greenland, Kent traveled far distances in search of landscapes. Many of the resulting canvases rival his earlier Alaskan scenes in their monumental ambition and engagement with the sublime. Although the settings are much alike, Kent had maintained an active social life in Greenland. Many of the resulting canvases include the inhabitants of this remote, isolated place, blending the grandeur of the landscapes with scenes of daily life. In doing so, Kent tempered the sublimity of this region with human presence.

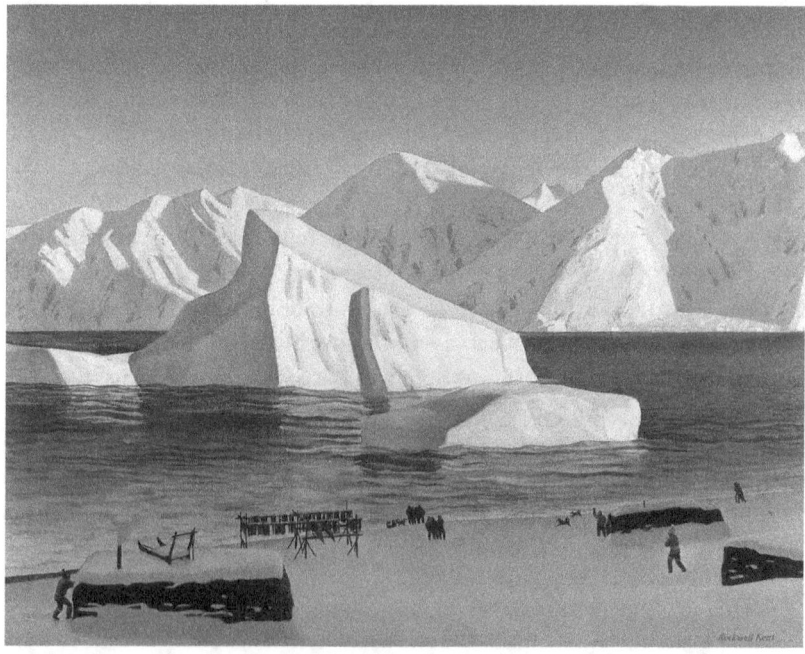

**Figure 24:** *Early November, North Greenland.* 1932. Oil on canvas. 86 × 110 cm. Hermitage Museum, Saint Petersburg.

CHAPTER 13

# Advocate (1933–1945)

When Kent had returned to Asgaard in 1932, he was shocked to learn that the Delaware and Hudson Railway had ceased passenger service from Plattsburgh to Au Sable Forks. This was more than an inconvenience in Kent's mind—it was a brazen betrayal. He asked the public service committee to investigate this issue. The hearings in Plattsburgh and Albany attracted a great deal of media attention. After a long fight, the service was restored. To Kent's distress, that victory was soon snatched away.

His battle to restore something lost reveals a key element in his character. He was quite willing—sometimes too willing—to wage war when he felt his rights had been trampled on. But he was also a fierce advocate for the rights of others. From early manhood, he held unyielding socialist principles.

For example, in August 1927, Nicola Sacco and Bartolomeo Vanzetti were executed for the killing of two men during an armed robbery in Braintree, Massachusetts in 1921. The case became controversial when evidence surfaced that they might not have been the culprits; in addition, it was obvious that anti-immigration, anti-Italian and anti-anarchist sentiments had been directed against them. Kent, convinced they were scapegoats, withdrew his participation in an exhibition there. He also vowed never to set foot again in Massachusetts.

Three years later, he quietly broke that vow when Raymond Moore, founder and impresario of the Cape Playhouse and Cinema in Dennis, Massachusetts contracted him to design murals for the cinema—including an extravagantly ambitious one for the ceiling. The work of transferring and painting Kent's cartoons was done by the set designer Jo Mielziner and a crew of stage set painters from New York City, but Kent traveled to Dennis in June 1930 to spend three days on the scaffolding making corrections.

# CHAPTER 13

In 1935, Kent was a celebrity who was quite willing to use that status in support for causes, especially those that defended the poor or those socially disadvantaged.

That November, a bitter strike took place at the Proctor Marble Company in Barre, Vermont. Kent had no doubts about the wrongs committed by the company: "I am appalled by the humility, the lack of manly pride, the slavish self-abasement of our working classes in that at the most they are fighting for is so little."[126] He spoke with the governor of Vermont, took part in a commission investigating the wretched living conditions of the workers, and donated money to what was in effect a doomed cause.

In general, he thought social conditions throughout the United States were horrific:

> Southern lynchings, the plight of the sharecroppers in the South…[the] arming of civilians against the peaceful lettuce-picket strikers … the Ku Klux Klan … nitwitted millions that the great American public school system has made just literate enough to read and swallow.[127]

Kent joined many activist groups because he believed his country was heading in perilous directions. His socialist beliefs led him to change "the name of what I believed in to Communism. Communism is coming. Capitalism is an outrageous, silly, cruel farce."[128] Despite those observations, he considered Roosevelt's New Deal offered a glimmer of hope. However, Communism, he felt, offered the best way forward, although he harbored deep reservations about joining the Party: "I have always had a strong suspicion that close personal association with Communists, particularly as a member of the Party, would be thoroughly disillusioning."[129]

Kent briefly revisited Alaska in 1935 to research the first ("Mail Service in the Arctic") of two panels for a mural commissioned by the Painting and Sculpture division of the Treasury department for installation at the new Post Office building at the Federal Triangle in Washington, D.C.; the following year he traveled to Puerto Rico to gather information for the companion panel ("Mail Service in the Tropics").

The first panel shows Inuit with dog and reindeer teams watching the departure of a mail plane; the second displays a group of Black Puerto Rican women receiving a letter written in Inuktitut. The glaring contrast between poor and rich in Puerto Rico stunned Kent. He came quickly to the conclusion that Puerto Rico should become independent. That resolution was heightened by the Ponce Massacre on March 21, 1937 when the police fired into a Nationalist demonstration killing 18 and wounding over a hundred. When they were unveiled in 1937, the murals aroused controversy when the Inuit script was translated. The message of the Inuit to the Puerto Ricans stated: "To the people of Puerto Rico, our friends. Go ahead, let us change our chiefs—that only will make us equal and free." To add insult to injury, conservative Puerto Rican politicians complained that the women on their panel were Black. When Kent's ploy of having the Inuit message contain revolutionary sentiments was discovered, the Treasury department threatened to withhold his fee of $2,500. The uproar ended when the wording was altered.

Back home, maintaining Asgaard was a constant preoccupation. In 1935, while she was staying in Arizona, Frances, without consulting her husband, rented Asgaard to a wealthy woman from Chicago. Outraged, he wrote the tenant that his home was "the repository of all my most precious and intimate possessions, of all the memorials of what has been most dear to me." It was "a most real and sacred place."[130] He insisted that the tenant should regard herself as his guest, requested she accept back her rent checks and not send anymore. When she refused to do so, he forwarded the total she paid him to the Communist Party of America. Kent's finances, always precarious, were briefly buoyed by a delayed inheritance from the Banker estate; soon afterwards, he lost that money in devastating stock market investments.

From the outset, running Asgaard was a money-losing proposition. There was a Jersey herd to look after and a bottling plant to oversee the running of "Asgaard Dairy Milk." In New York City, he met a young man who improbably claimed to be Prince Michael Dimitri Romanoff, a member of the Russian nobility. Not really taken in by the charade, Kent nevertheless offered him room and board for performing routine chores at Asgaard. The Prince proved to be shiftless and soon ran away with his host's driving license and check book. A few weeks later, he surfaced in Arizona and California as Rockwell Kent, much to the artist's astonishment and grim amusement.

To raise much-needed income, Kent had in 1933 gone on a national lecture tour. In 1937, he reluctantly did so again. Although he was a brilliant

## CHAPTER 13

performer with considerable charisma and candor, he detested the grueling timetable of rail travel and brief overnight stays. He also flirted with Hollywood, exploring various dream projects that, as Jake Milgram Wien has shown, he hoped might prove lucrative.[131]

In order to make ends meet, Kent maintained a rigorous work schedule of working on canvases, book illustrations, and advertisements. Even so, social activism often pulled him away from his easel.

Reluctantly, Kent, as President of the National Committee for Peoples' Rights, traveled to Brazil to investigate the reported torture and imprisonments enacted by the regime of Getúlio Vargas. On his first night in Rio de Janeiro, he and a colleague were taken in the middle of the night by the police for questioning. Realizing the raw, unaccountable power of his interrogators, Kent played the role of the saintly fool. After this frightening incident, the two Americans were allowed to continue their investigation.

Back home, Kent in his report maintained that Vargas might be a dictator, but that he was not a fascist. "Unconstitutional though the Vargas coup d'etat had been, dictatorial as was his power, and ruthlessly repressive of minorities and civil liberties in general as he had shown himself to be, his was no more that purposefully integrated, totalitarian despotism of a class which is properly to be termed Fascism than—leaping to the present—is our America today. Democracy? Not by a long sight. But Fascism? No; not quite." When the sponsors of his trip did not agree with this verdict, they rewrote his findings. Kent exploded; his findings were eventually restored.

In 1939, Kent began writing *This is My Own* (1940). This book is an account of his life at Asgaard, but into it he poured his views on socialism and the failures of the American dream. That year, he was called to testify before congressman Martin Dies Jr.'s Special Committee to Investigate Un-American Activities. At that confrontation, he truthfully denied membership in the Communist Party.

Kent's marriage to Frances had waned considerably by 1940. He had been furious at her decision to rent Asgaard without consulting him. She also made it quite clear to her husband that the preferred places like Florida and Arizona to the cold climates to which he was attracted. In January 1940, Kent hired twenty-five-year-old English-born Sally Johnston to work for him as an assistant. Soon afterwards, he was in her rapturous thrall:

## ADVOCATE (1933–1945)

It wasn't easy when every hour that we were together—the hour or more of dictation, our meals together, our times outdoors when, shutting shop, we'd wander through the woods on snowshoes or go skiing on the pasture hills, and our long evenings at the fireside where, conversing, I delighted in her thoughts, her voice, her crystal clear enunciation—it wasn't easy when every word of hers and every motion, every look, endeared her more to me. In fact it soon became so far from easy that in a few days I just gave up trying. And driving her one lovely afternoon to the foot of a high hill, floundering afoot with her through the deep snow to the top, and there revealing to her enraptured eyes the whole wonderland of that North Country world, I said to her—almost in these very words—"all this will I give thee, if thou wilt fall down and worship me." So next day Sally packed her things and left.

Beside himself with anxiety, he waited a week before phoning her: "And in her answer—no matter, I've forgotten her words—in the ardor, love, and poignant need of me her voice conveyed there spoke the promise of which our happiness throughout the years has been the fulfillment."[132]

Kent did not want his break with his 41-year-old wife to be bitter. "Frances, though bound for Arizona, had lingered in New York. I asked her to return. And here at Asgaard she met Sally—met her and took her to her heart. Out of the deep goodness of a heart that in that crisis let her only think of me, she gave us two her blessing." Frances and Kent ended their 14 year marriage that year; in May, Kent married for the third time.

When Kent fell in love with Sally, his passion was, as usual, all-consuming. That was the paradigm that applied to all his romances. Although he was fully aware that Sally was about the same age as his daughter, Kathleen, he did not take into account that a relationship with a younger woman allowed him to assume control. His relationship with Frances fell apart when she made decisions contrary to his expectations. She had been Sally's age—twenty-six—when they wed.

When war broke out in 1941, Kent fully supported the American war efforts. In addition, he was concerned with the fate of the Soviet people, especially the devastating siege of Leningrad that began in September 1941. Kent's allegiance was to the United States, but he felt a strong connection to *what he knew* of how socialism was practiced in the USSR. For him, "the attack upon the Soviet Union opened a struggle between opposing ideologies upon whose outcome rested mankind's future for years to come." Skepticism about the USSR had to be pushed aside: "That belief in the Soviet Union ... for which so many had been persecuted—was now in time of need to prove its usefulness."[133]

## CHAPTER 13

As he later recalled, "in 1940, not even with Sally at my side, was the world—for me, for us, for anyone—that good."[134] Kent contributed to the war effort in a variety of ways. He curated the 1942–1943 traveling exhibition *Know and Defend America: Forty Paintings of Our Country and of the Out-posts of Our Hemisphere*. At Asgaard, he expanded his dairy operations by adding to his Jersey herd and by opening a bottling plant. He made posters in support of the war effort.

One of Kent's most poignant statements about the war is the brightly colored landscape *December Eight, 1941* (1941)—also called *The Open Road*. [The title refers to the bombing of Pearl Harbor]. Three figures at the door on the right stare mournfully ahead; at the fence, a young woman waves to a figure in the distance—a mere speck—presumably her brother, lover or husband. The landscape vividly pictures the beauty of the American landscape, the survival of which sends the young man off to war. In the catalog of *Know and Defend America*, Kent reflected on this canvas: "the road that led out into a wider world has been open for many generations, and youth has taken it, and more youth now in these days will take it. And many, because of what will happen to them, will never return."

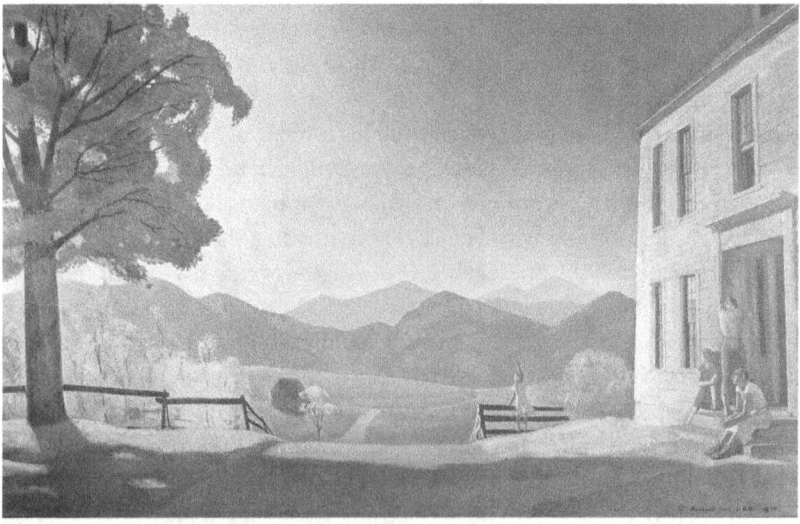

**Figure 25:** *December Eight, 1941 (The Open Road)*. 1941. Oil on canvas. 109 × 180 cm. Plattsburgh State Art Museum.

CHAPTER 14

# Politico (1945–1971)

The aftermath of war was far from what Kent had yearned for. "[T]he struggle for the survival of those very principles"[135] for which the great conflict had been fought seemed to be in grave doubt. The nation seemed to have turned blue "so cold, so hostile" had it become to democracy.[136]

In 1942, Kent had written to back the typographers at R. R. Donnelly's Lakeside Press—where *Moby Dick* had been printed—in their efforts to unionize.

> The one thing above all others that America prides itself upon is the high standard of living of its people. And by people we mean the workers.…if these workers and their families enjoy good living it is because the workers, through organization, have won good wages for themselves. It is organized labor in America that has won, for all Americans, the right to be proud of their country.

He also saw himself as a "worker, in that I earn my living by the work I do … I have worked at lots of trades in the course of my life. If they were organized I joined. If they were not organized I worked to organize them."[137] He wrote an "electrifying letter" that supported the typographers. Furious at Kent's intervention, Donnelly's refused to participate in what would have been a magnificent project—a Bible illustrated by Kent.

After Franklin Delano Roosevelt's death in April 1945, Kent felt that pro-Fascist forces in the United States were gaining the upper hand. In Kent's opinion, Henry Wallace and the Progressive Party offered the best hope for continuing Roosevelt's New Deal. For that reason, in 1948, Kent ran unsuccessfully for Congress as an American Labor Party candidate supporting Henry Wallace's presidential bid for the Progressive Party.

CHAPTER 14

At the onset of the Cold War, Kent not only supported Soviet Russia but also nuclear disarmament. Five years earlier, he had been summoned before Martin Dies' Un-American Activities committee, and well before the end of the war, he was a known supporter of liberal causes. When he printed "Vote for Wallace" inside the bottle caps of Asgaard Dairy Milk and distributed broadsides to support him, long-time customers refused to buy what they derisively called "Red Milk." Kent retired from selling it and turned over the dairy to two employees.

The onset of the Cold War can be clearly seen in *Heavy, Heavy Hangs Over They Head* (1946–1949) in which the sleeping baby references the Newfoundland painting *My Daughter Clara* (1930). In the earlier painting, the landscape behind the baby is filled with dark browns and somber blues. The contrast in *Heavy* is much more stark. While the baby sleeps under a rifle, a mouse gnaws at the cord attached to a nail above her head.

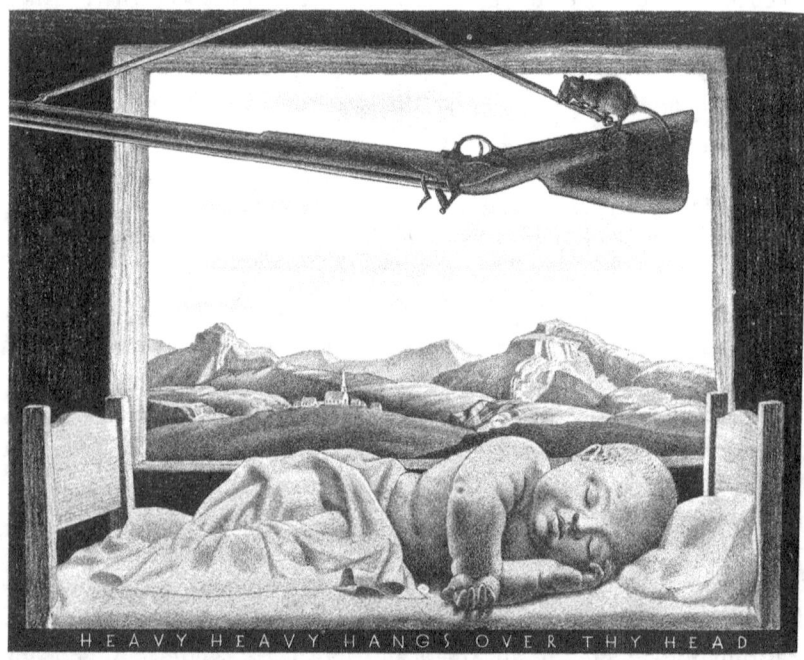

**Figure 26:** *Heavy, Heavy Hangs over Thy Head.* 1946. Lithograph. 23 × 30 cm. Metropolitan Museum of Art.

Kent became vividly aware that anti-liberal forces were flourishing even in unexpected places. In 1947, two years after the end of the war, Kent revisited Monhegan. That same year, his mother, the indomitable Sara Kent, died. Perhaps to rekindle and reimagine his earliest years as an artist, he repurchased and repaired his house on Monhegan the following year.

> The little house on Monhegan—yes, we bought it back; one is apt to get things that one wants a lot—the little house proved to be in deplorable condition; and Sally and I, on our return there in the spring, spent virtually every hour of our month of ten or twelve hour working days pulling out nails from plaster walls and wooden trim, scraping and scrubbing, patching and painting—and, outdoors, digging, grubbing, chopping, lopping—so that at our vacation's end we ... had a place that was almost fit to live in.

By 1953, Kent's visits to Monhegan became increasingly fraught. He was a public figure who was suspected of being a Communist. After two FBI agents called on them in the town, Sally remembered: "How sad we were as suspicions grew on the part of our close friends ... We recognized the symptoms promptly: avoidance on the footpaths, hurried departures from the store when we appeared."[138] Despite happy memories of his past in Monhegan, he came to the conclusion that he could no longer live there. He sold the house and never returned to the island.

Kent's participation in the Stockholm Appeal and the World Peace Council led to the suspension of his passport in 1950. In 1951 he came under attack for his role as an officer in the International Workers Order, a fraternal, mutual benefit organization formed in 1930 that provided medical and life insurance to immigrants and low-income workers. It was closely associated with the Communist Party, but, as historian Arthur J. Sabin has noted, "In reality, most members were attracted to the low cost and non-discriminatory availability of insurance and the willingness to take on as insureds anyone who worked, even those who worked in dangerous or high risk employment, as well as the mutual aid benefits of the Order .... That it was also dedicated to left-wing, "progressive," or indeed Party-supported causes and rhetoric cannot and should not be ignored or glossed over; nevertheless, for most of its members, the IWO met pragmatic needs in an economic and social framework."[139] Kent defended himself in court and maintained accurately that he was not a member of the Communist Party.

## CHAPTER 14

In 1953, he was subpoenaed to appear before Joseph McCarthy's Permanent Subcommittee on Investigation. The acerbic McCarthy inquired why Kent had donated $900 to the Communist Party in 1935. Kent responded that he had wanted to offend the rich woman who had paid that amount, against his will, to rent Asgaard. The Senator then asked if Kent had ever belonged to the Communist Party, whereupon Kent invoked the Fifth Amendment. In turn, McCarthy asserted that Kent was obviously a Communist. The artist then asked if he could give a statement for the record. McCarthy brushed him aside: "I'm not going to listen to a lecture from you." Kent retorted: "You're not going to get one. I get paid for my lectures." As he left the hearing, Kent proclaimed: "I'm sorry. I had serious charges to bring here of a conspiracy to overthrow the government by force and violence." Outside the hearing room, Kent distributed copies of a statement claiming that McCarthy was the leader of a conspiracy to topple "our Democracy in favor of a Fascist, totalitarian government."

Earlier in 1953, en route back from painting on Monhegan, Kent had called at the Farnsworth Museum in Rockland to discuss a possible exhibition of his paintings. The Director was sufficiently enthusiastic about that proposal that Kent asked if the Farnsworth would be interested in accepting Kent's own large collection of his work. That proposal excited the Director, who said he would take this matter up with his trustees and suggested that a new wing might be added to accommodate the donation. When Kent arrived back at Asgaard from Washington, he found a letter from the Director: There would be no exhibition; the proposed donation would not be accepted.

The market for Kent's paintings began to evaporate. One reason for this turning was the rise of abstract art in Europe and, in the United States, Abstract Expressionism, an art form fervently promoted by various government agencies. For him, "Abstraction [was] the cultural counterpart of the atom bomb."[140] Speaking of the New York art establishment, Kent was a bit less strident:

> The sappy New York critics keep yapping that it is the duty of the artist to be Modern, that Modernism is New York today, and that art should be a paean to steel, noise, jazz and its vulgarities. Of course art can be that. But it seems to me that if the artist has any real historical function it is to preserve the consciousness of the

deeper and more enduring values of life against such threats of disintegration as our rampant city Modernism holds.[141]

Although critics dismissed these remarks as merely reactionary, this is not so. Under the tutelage of Henri, Kent had become the advocate of a distinctly American form of modernism. In his Newfoundland, Alaska, Tierra del Fuego and Greenland landscapes he had incorporated passages that are decidedly abstract. Kent was not so much hostile to the popularity of a movement such as Abstract Expressionism as he wanted to assert that his practice as an artist had been "to preserve the consciousness of the deeper and more endearing values of life." In this instance, he had incorporated ideas of transcendence in landscapes that are representational. For him, there was many paths to the palace of art.

Kent inherited $30,000 from his mother in 1947 and placed it in the hands of a reliable broker who quickly doubled and then tripled it. This considerably eased his financial situation. Further assistance came from Joseph James Ryan, the grandson of the financier, Thomas Fortune Ryan. A great admirer of Kent's—and, like him, a fierce opponent of the diminishment of the freedoms stomped on in post war United States—was perturbed by right-wing slurs on the artist. Of an eccentric turn, Ryan flew to Asgaard in a giant B-17 bomber he had converted into a private plane. On that visit, he bought six paintings. He subsequently purchased many more and commissioned others.

In 1955, Kent published his voluminous (over 600 pages, 94 chapters) autobiography *It's Me O Lord* in which, with considerable poise, he recounted his life. Ten years earlier, in *This is My Own*, he had dwelled on his discovery of Asgaard, the lawsuit against the Delaware and Hudson Railway, and the Eden-like atmosphere of Asgaard. Both books are brimful of anecdotes in which the narrator emerges successfully from trying situations; confesses his sexual adventures; describes the outset of his career as an artist and the obstacles he steadfastly overcame; relates, in a self-congratulatory manner, his confrontations with officialdom. In both books, the writer forms a bond with his audience as he recounts the trials and tribulations that beset him. Both narratives may be infused with the author's charisma, but they contain very little introspection. Kent established his own point of view but failed to pay heed to opinions that conflicted with his own.

## CHAPTER 14

From 1957 to 1971, Kent served as president of the National Council of American-Soviet Friendship. After he filed suit to regain his foreign-travel rights, in June 1958, the U.S. Supreme Court in Kent vs. Dulles affirmed Kent's right to travel by declaring the ban a violation of his civil rights. After a well-received exhibition of his work in five Soviet museums—Pushkin State Museum of Fine Arts, the State Hermitage Museum, Kiev Museum of Western and Eastern Art, Odessa Museum of Western and Eastern Art and State Museum of Fine Arts, Riga—in 1957-1958, he donated several hundred of his paintings and drawings to the Soviet peoples in 1960. The donation was made in large part because of the Farnsworth's decision in 1953 not to accept what would have been essentially the same works.

Kent subsequently became an honorary member of the Soviet Academy of Fine Arts and in 1967 the recipient of the International Lenin Peace Prize. Kent specified that $20,000 of his prize money be given to the women and children of both North and South Vietnam. That award gained Kent condemnation by the media in the United States, by his congressman, and by individuals who sent him hate mail. Kent's "prints and drawings were used for Soviet depictions of Kent as a Socialist. For instance, Soviet newspapers often featured Kent's print *Workers of the World Unite!*."[142]

From Newfoundland, Joey Smallwood, the Premier, offered a formal apology for the way he had been branded a German spy 50 years before and invited him to return as a guest of his government. That offer was gladly accepted.

Into his seventies, Kent's health was marred only by bouts with kidney stones and gallstones. In 1962, he suffered a cerebral stroke that paralyzed the left side of his body. He recovered, but then his heartbeat slowed considerably. A pacemaker was implanted in 1965. Always a person to speak his mind stridently—even rudely, he became even more sharp tongued and irritable. He wrote, drew and painted as much as he could in trying circumstances.

The landscapes created at Asgaard may not be as overtly symbolical or transcendent as the various wilderness landscapes, but their tranquility, resplendent colors and celebration of the natural world as in *Asgaard Meadows* (1946) call to mind the kind of celebration seen in Edward Hicks's *Peaceable Kingdom* (1834).

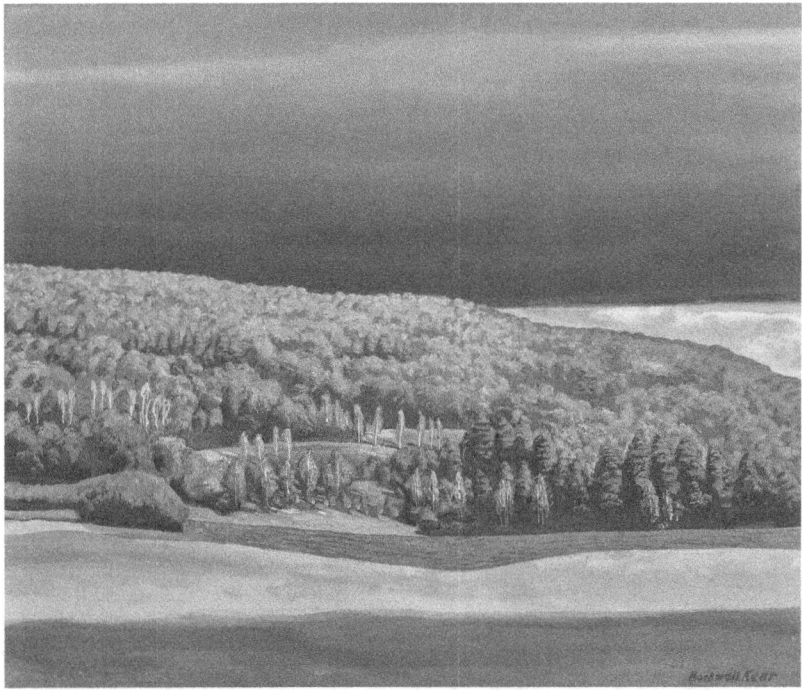

**Figure 27:** *Golden Autumn.* c. 1955. Oil on canvas. 71 × 86 cm. Private Collection.

Asgaard remained Kent's refuge. In a cool spring night in 1969, lighting struck the house. Sally drove to the telephone office to put in an alarm. When she returned, her husband was sitting in their Chevy station wagon watching the volunteer fire fighters battle the blaze. At first, Kent thought the house could be rescued. At one point, he even entered the house and retrieved a favorite Greenland canvas. Unfortunately, the fire regained control and completely demolished everything in its path.

The next day, Kent began drawing plans for a new Asgaard. He and Sally moved to a two room cottage attached to their barn. By summer, a smaller house was ready. The following year his health worsened. A new pacemaker was installed, but his energy was eaten up. Insomnia and nightmares tormented him. On March 2, 1971, he became unconscious and was taken to the hospital in Plattsburgh, where he died on March 13 at the age of 88.

# Epilogue by Way of Four Self-Portraits

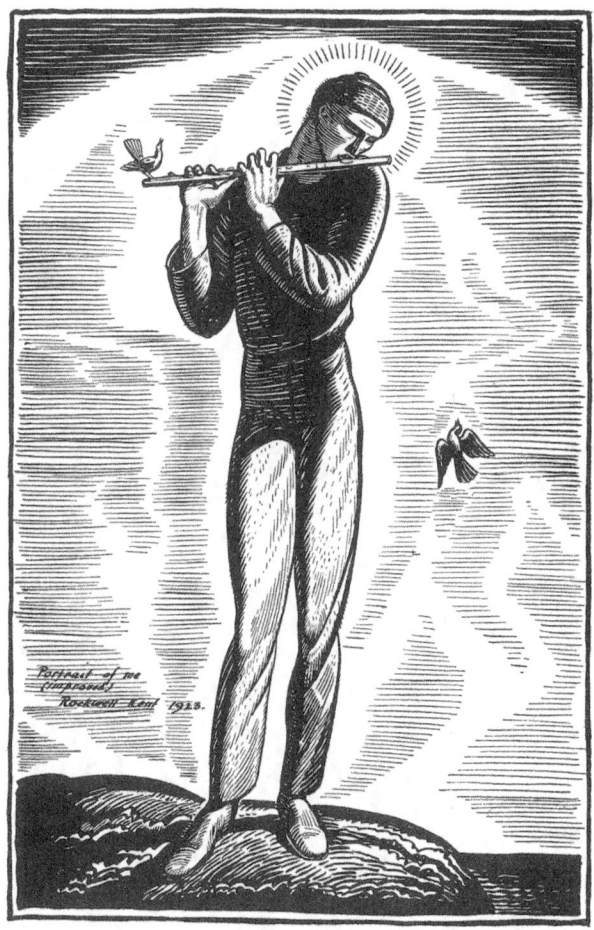

**Figure 28:** *Portrait of Me Improved*. Frontispiece to *Voyaging*. 1924. Private Collection.

## EPILOGUE BY WAY OF FOUR SELF-PORTRAITS

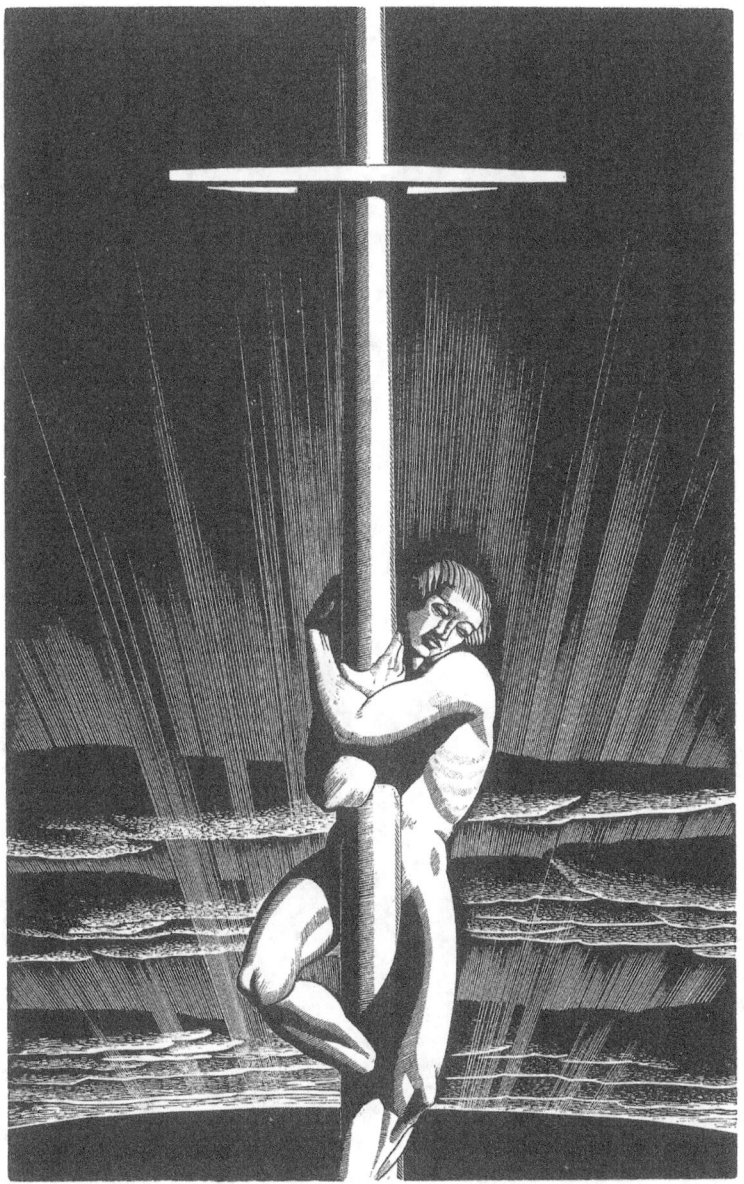

**Figure 29:** *Sea and Sky*. Wood engraving. 1931–1932. 25.4 × 17 cm. Private Collection.

# EPILOGUE BY WAY OF FOUR SELF-PORTRAITS

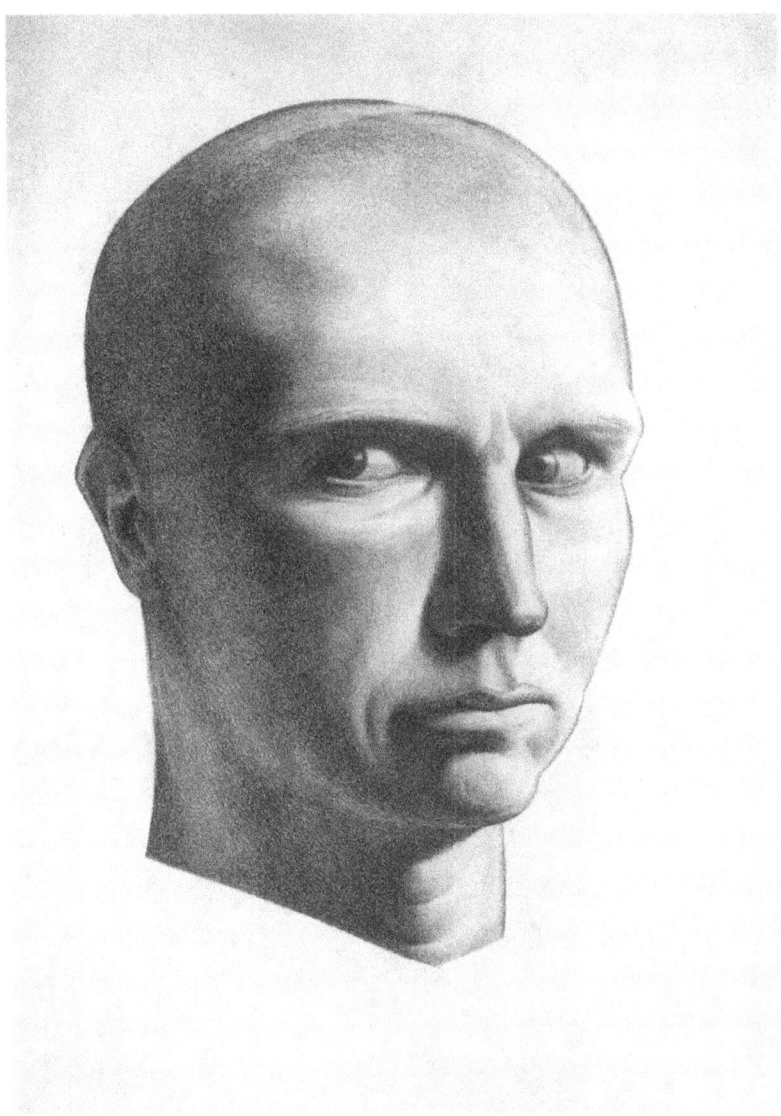

**Figure 30:** *Self-Portrait*. Lithograph on stone. 1934. 35 × 25.4 cm. Private Collection.

# EPILOGUE BY WAY OF FOUR SELF-PORTRAITS

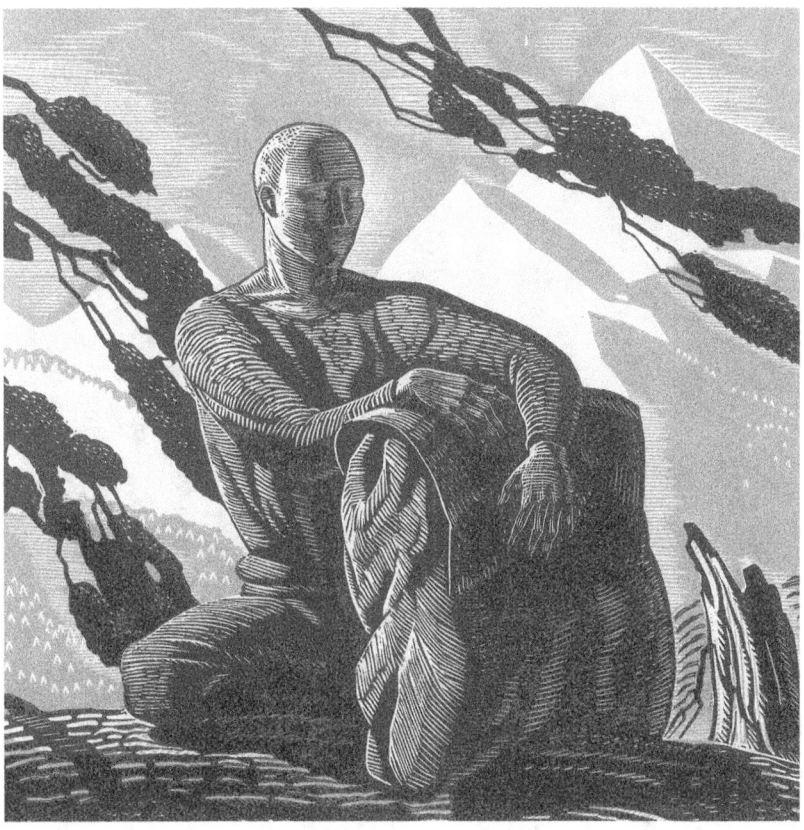

**Figure 31:** Self-portrait. *Voyaging*. 1924. Color woodcut. 15 × 15 cm. Private Collection.

## EPILOGUE BY WAY OF FOUR SELF-PORTRAITS

From an early age, Rockwell Kent's life was marked by turbulence. He found his greatest sense of peace and purpose in solitude, a condition that became essential to his art. Kent was deeply influenced by mystical ideas and the Transcendentalist movement. Equally important to him was sexual connection, and his romantic impulses often pulled him in conflicting directions.

Kent was aware of these contradictions within himself. One side of him was poetic and reflective, captured in his wood engraving *Portrait of Me Improved* (1924). There, he carries a flute, a testament to his lasting attachment to the memory of his father.

His wood engraving *Sea and Sky* (1931–1932) reveals a more troubled aspect of his nature. During his years in Newfoundland and Alaska, Kent confronted his own deep insecurities—here he depicts himself literally hanging on for dear life.

The same inner turmoil appears in his *Self-Portrait* (1934), which presents the face of an apprehensive, even tortured man, glancing anxiously to the side. In contrast, the color wood engraving in *Voyaging* (1924) shows a muscular seated figure holding a rucksack. This man seems to be in quiet contemplation, perhaps charting the next stage of a personal voyage. His body is revealed in full detail, but his face is masked—his eyes blank, his features expressionless.

In many ways, Kent remained a stranger to himself. Self-assured in manner yet riven by inner conflict, he stumbled often in love, though his social conscience seldom wavered. At heart, he remained the lost little boy of his youth. It was in the act of creating art of enduring worth that the man discovered himself.

# Short Titles and Abbreviations

AAA
Archives of American Art

*IMOL*
*It's Me O Lord: The Autobiography of Rockwell Kent* (New York, Dodd, Mead & Company, 1955)

RK
Rockwell Kent

Traxel
*An American Saga: The Life and Times of Rockwell Kent* (New York: Harper & Row, 1980)

Wien
Jake Milgram Wien, *Rockwell Kent: The Mythic and the Modern* (Manchester: Hudson Hills Press, 2005)

# Endnotes

1 Quoted in C. Lewis Hind, "Rockwell Kent in Alaska and Elsewhere," *International Studio*, vol. 67, no. 268 (June 1919), p. 112.
2 Merle Armitage, *Rockwell Kent* (New York: Alfred A. Knopf, 1932), p. 2.
3 Ibid., p. 44.
4 Ibid. 7–8.
5 Quoted by Armitage. p. 29.
6 Ibid.
7 *IMOL*, p. 1.
8 Letter from Sally Gorton Kent to David Traxel April 25, 1974.
9 *IMOL*, p. 15
10 Ibid.
11 *IMOL* p. 59.
12 Ibid., p. 36.
13 Sally Gorton Kent provided this information to David Traxel on February 28, 1974.
14 *IMOL*, p. 50.
15 Ibid., p. 51.
16 Ibid., p. 80.
17 Ibid., pp. 76–7.
18 *IMOL*, pp. 82–3.
19 Bernard B. Perlman, *The Immortal Eight: American Painting from Eakins to the Armory Show (1870–1913)* (New York: North Light Publishers, 1962), pp. 117, 115, 24.
20 *IMOL*, pp. 100–1.
21 Ibid., pp 96–7.
22 *IMOL*, p. 118.
23 Ibid., p. 120.
24 Kent to Henri, July 12, 1905. RH archive.
25 *IMOL*, p. 122.
26 Ibid.
27 Ibid.
28 Quoted by Michael Kimmel in *Angry White Men: American Masculinity at the End of an Era* (New York: Nation Books, 2013), p. 101

ENDNOTES

29 *IMOL*, p. 109.
30 Kimmel, p. 116.
31 "The New York Exhibition of Independent Artists," *Craftsman* 18, no 2 (May 1910), p. 162.
32 April 5, 1907.
33 "True American Art in Kent's Pictures." *New York American*, April 3, 1907.
34 Wien, p. 30.
35 Jake Milgram Wien, "Rockwell Kent and Edward Hopper: Looking Out, Looking Within," *The Magazine Antiques*, February 26, 2016.
36 "At the Galleries," *Saturday Evening Post*, March 3, 1917.
37 *IMOL* p. 169.
38 Ibid., pp. 99–200.
39 Ibid., p. 155.
40 Ibid., p. 200.
41 RK to Kathleen Kent, July 2, 1910. AAA.
42 Ibid.
43 *IMOL*, p. 62.
44 Ibid., p. 199.
45 Ibid., p. 244.
46 Kathleen Kent to RK, October 11, 1911. AAA.
47 Ibid.
48 *IMOL*, p. 225.
49 "There can be little question that personal elements [made this exhibition a center of conflict]. Kent's driving, aggressive personality could become abrasive when he was excited. According to [John] Sloan, Henri was angered by Kent's language and the manner in which he laid down the conditions under which an artist could enter the exhibit." Traxel, p. 61. Although Henri became angry at Kent's attempt to seize control of the Independent Group, that resentment did not last long.
50 *IMOL*, p. 241.
51 Robert Pearmain to Kent, May 12, 1912. AAA.
52 *IMOL*, p. 236.
53 Ibid.
54 *IMOL*, p. 252.
55 Ibid., p. 296.
56 Ibid.
57 Ibid.
58 Ibid., p. 289.
59 RK to Charles Daniel, January 8, 1915. Kent Papers, University of Virginia.
60 Jake Milgram Wien, "Mystery as Beauty: Rockwell Kent's Symbolist Theatre" in Jamie Franklin and Jake Milgram Wien, *Rockwell Kent's "Egypt": Shadow and Light in Vermont* (Bennington: Bennington Museum: 2012), p. 21.
61 RK to Charles Daniel, January 8, 1916. Kent Papers University of Virginia.
62 "Newfoundland as Pictured by Rockwell Kent's Imagination," *New York American*, March 1917.

## ENDNOTES

63 Charles Daniel to RK, January 25, 1915. AAA.
64 *IMOL*, p. 306.
65 Wien, p. 85.
66 *IMOL*, p. 308.
67 Wien, pp. 89–90.
68 RK to Hildegarde Hirsch, undated. Cited in "His Mind on Fire: Rockwell Kent's Amorous Letters to Hildegarde Hirsch and Ernesta Drinker Bullitt, 1916–1925," *Columbia Library Columns* (Autumn 1997), p. 9. This seminal article contains much new documentary information on Kent. I have relied on it in discussing Kent's relationships with Hirsch and Bullitt.
69 *IMOL*, p. 319.
70 Ibid., pp. 319–20.
71 Kent to Kathleen Kent, n.d. but probably June 14, 1917. AAA.
72 *IMOL*, p. 325.
73 RK to Hildegarde Hirsch, December 2, 1918. AAA. Cited by Wien, "His Mind on Fire," p. 12.
74 *IMOL*, p. 332.
75 *IMOL*, p. 335.
76 *Wilderness: A Journal of Quiet Adventure in Alaska* (New York: The Modern Library, 1930), p. 97.
77 RK to Carl Zigrosser, Jan 24, 1919.
78 RK to Carl Zigrosser, December 3, 1918.
79 *Wilderness*, p. 107.
80 RK to Kathleen Kent, December 18, 1918. AAA.
81 RK to Carl Zigrosser, October 23, 1918.
82 *IMOL*, p. 337.
83 RK to Kathleen Kent, December 3 and 8, 1918. AAA.
84 RK to Kathleen Kent, December 25, 1918. AAA.
85 RK to Kathleen Kent, February 16, 1919. AAA.
86 RK to CZ, March 8, 1919. AAA.
87 *IMOL*, p. 338.
88 RK to Carl Zigrosser, November 23, 1918.
89 RK to Ferdinand Howald, February 19, 1919.
90 May 11, 1919.
91 *IMOL*, p. 342.
92 *My Own Shall Come to Me: A Personal Memoir and Picture* Chronicle (Haarlam, Casa Laura, 1971), p. 4.
93 RK to Howald, April 11, 1920.
94 RK to Howald, August 24, 1920.
95 *IMOL*, p. 355.
96 Carl Zigrosser to RK. AAA.
97 *IMOL*, p. 356.
98 At this time, Kent severed his ties with Marie Sterner and made Martin Birnbaum his agent until he and Gerald Kelly, director of exhibitions at Wildenstein Gallery, concluded a formal agreement for Wildenstein to represent him.

ENDNOTES

99   Furlong to Chappell, April 31, 1922.
100  *IMOL*, p. 358.
101  *IMOL*, pp. 364–5.
102  F. D. De Witt Wells to "Morgan," May 23, 1924. Cited by Traxel, p. 230.
103  *IMOL*, p. 397.
104  Ibid., pp. 400–1.
105  Ibid., pp. 401–2.
106  RK to Ernesta Drinker, undated.
107  Ibid., p. 413.
108  Ibid., p. 430.
109  "Ideas on Decorating" (1940). Cited by Caroline M. Welsh, "Rockwell Kent: A Life and Art of His Own," in Catherine M. Welsh and Scott R. Ferris, *The View from Asgaard: Rockwell Kent's Adirondack Legacy* (Blue Mountain Lake: The Adirondack Museum, 1999), p. 12.
110  Rockwell Kent, *This is My Own* (New York: Duell, Sloan and Pearce, 1940), p. 143.
111  *IMOL*, p. 439.
112  *IMOL*, p. 398.
113  Ibid.
114  Ibid., p. 430.
115  Ibid., p. 438.
116  *At Random: The Reminiscences of Bennett Cerf* (New York: Random House, 2002), p. 72
117  Reproduced in Eliot H. Stanley, *Rediscovering Rockwell Kent: Books, Graphics and Decorative Arts* (New York: Grolier Club, 1997), p. 19.
118  Heritage Club Sandglass
119  Anonymous, "Caught on the Run," August 4, 1904, *Duluth New Tribune*.
120  *IMOL*, p. 439.
121  Ibid., p. 441.
122  Ibid., p. 452.
123  Ibid., p. 454.
124  Ibid., p. 455.
125  Ibid., p. 477.
126  Letter in *New Masses*, January 31, 1936. AAA.
127  RK to Sydney Lowenthal, September 1936. AAA.
128  RK to Stuart Davis, January 27, 1936. AAA.
129  RK to Hans, April 11, 1950. AAA.
130  Draft of letter to Mrs. Blair, July 28, 1935. AAA.
131  "Rockwell Kent and Hollywood," *Archives of American Art Journal*, volume 42, numbers 1–4, 2002.
132  *IMOL*, p. 530.
133  Ibid., p. 542.
134  Ibid., p. 535.
135  *IMOL*, p. 568.
136  Ibid.
137  Ibid., p. 566.

# ENDNOTES

138 Sally Gorton Kent in *The Kent Collector*, Winter 1977.
139 Arthur *Sabin, Red Scare in Court: New York versus the International Workers Order*, (Philadelphia: University of Pennsylvania Press), 1993.
140 Letter to editor of *New York Times Magazine*, December 30, 1952.
141 Letter to Bayard Boyesen, January 7, 1936. AAA.
142 Kirill Chunikhin, "At Home Among Strangers: U.S. Artists, the Soviet Union, and the Myth of Rockwell Kent during the Cold War," *Journal of Cold War Studies* 21, no 4 (Fall 2019), p. 195.

# Index

Page numbers in **bold** indicate the reproduction if a work of art

abstract art 106-7
Adam and Eve 46
Admiralty Sound, Tierra del Fuego 77
Alaskan Territory (later Alaska) 4, 98
Albany, New York 97
American art 13-4, 39
American Labor Party 103
Antaeus 26-7
Arlington, Vermont 70
Armitage, Merle 2-4
Armory Show (International Exhibition of Modern Art) 32
Art Students League 13
Asgaard, RK's home in the Adirondacks 83-4, 92, 97, 99, 107-9
Asgaard Dairy Milk 99, 104
Ashcan School of Art 13, 39
Au Sable Forks, New York 83, 97

Baddock, Nova Scotia 84, 93
Banker, James, Sara Kent's uncle 7-8
Banker, Josie, Sara Kent's aunt 7, 19
*A Basket of Poses* **45**
Bellows, George 13, 20
Bennington, Vermont 70
*Beowulf* 86
Blake, William 38, 52-3; *Book of Job* 66, 70
Boccaccio *The Decameron* 86
Boston, Massachusetts 29-30
Brazil 100
*The Bricklayer* 44
Brigus, Newfoundland 35-7
Brigus Tennis Club 35-6
Bullitt, William C. 81

Burin, Newfoundland 29, 35
Butler, Samuel, *Erewhon* 86
Caffin, Charles 40
Cape Horn, Tierra del Fuego, Chile 77
Cape Playhouse and Cinema, Dennis, Massachusetts 97
Caritas Island, Long Island Sound, Connecticut 24
Casanova, *Memoirs* 85-6
Cerf, Bennett 85
Chaplin, Charlie 44
Chappell. George 17, 43-4, 75
Chase, William Merritt 12-3, 14
Chaucer, *Canterbury Tales* 85-6
Claussen Galleries 19
Cold War 104
Columbia University 12-3
Communist Party 105-6
Community House and Library, Pocantico Hills, New York 14
Conception Bay, Newfoundland 35
Coomaraswamy, Ananda 52-3
Crestalban, Lanesborough, Massachusetts 23
Crowninshield, Frank 44
Cubism 32, 39
*Curaca* 77

Dana Jr., Richard Henry, *Two Years Before the Mast* 77, 86
David Copperfield 5
Daniel, Charles 32, 37, 40, 43, 47
Davies, Arthur B. 30
Delaware and Hudson Railway 97, 107

INDEX

Dies Jr., Martin 100, 104
*Direction* 84, 93-4
*Disco* 94
R. B. Donnelly 103
Dow, Arthur Wesley 13
Drinker, Ernesta 81-2, 85
Dublin, New Hampshire 14, 18, 23, 31
Duchamp, Marcel, *Nude Descending a Staircase* 32; *Fountain* 48

Earhart, Emilia 76
"Egypt," Kent's home in Vermont 70-1, 83
Emerson, Ralph Waldo 3, 13-4, 24
Enehøje, Denmark 95
Englewood School 71
Episcopal Academy, Cheshire, Connecticut 11
Ericson, Leif 79
Ewing, Charles 17
Ewing and Chappell 17, 24, 30, 32, 43
*Exhibition of the American Society of Independent Artists* 47-8

Farnsworth Museum, Rockland, Maine 106
Faroe Islands, Denmark 94
Fisher, Dorothy Canfield 70-1
Fisher, John 70
Fishermen's Protective Union 35
Fox Island, Resurrection Bay, Alaska 51-2, 55-6
Freuchen, Peter 94
Frick, Henry Clay 48
Fuller, Margaret 13
Furlong, Charles Wellington 76

Gauguin, Paul 39
Godhavn, Greenland 95

Godthaab, Greenland 93-4
Goethe, *Faust* 86
Grand Bank, Newfoundland 29
Greenland 4, 84, 92-6
Green Mountains, Vermont 70
Greenwich, Connecticut 71-2
Greenwich Village 26, 31, 43

*Harper's Weekly* 44
Hartley, Marsden 31, 33
Henri, Robert 13-5, 17-8, 24, 27, 30, 39, 48
Hercules 26-7, 91
Heritage Press 87
Hirsch, Frieda 46
Hirsch, Hildegarde 46-8, 51, 66, 79
Hodler, Ferdinand 38
Holgate, Josephine (Jo) RK's aunt 11, 80
Homer, Winslow 19
Hopper, Edward 20
Horace Mann School, New York City 12
Horn's Hill, Monhegan 19
Huneker, James, *The Sun* 19

Ibsen, Henrik 39
Igdlorssuit, Ubekendt Island, Greenland 94-5
*An Independent Exhibition of the Paintings and Drawings of Twelve Men* 30
Industrial Workers of the World 31
International Workers Order 105
Ireland 4
Irvington, New York 7-8

James, Henry, *The Bostonians* 18
*Judge* 46
Juneau, Alaska 51

# INDEX

*Kathleen I* 77
*Kathleen II* 77
Kent, Barbara, RK's daughter 35, 47
Kent, Clara, RK's daughter 30, 32, 47
Kent, Douglas, RK's brother 8
Kent, Frances Lee Higgins, RK's second wife 82, 94-6
Kent, George Rockwell, RK's father 7-9, 56
Kent, Gordon, RK's son 71, 95-6
Kent, Karl, RK's son 30
Kent, Kathleen Whiting, RK's first wife 23-5, 30, 32, 46-7, 66-7, 69-71, 75, 77, 78-81
Kent, Kathleen, RK's daughter 30, 47

**KENT, ROCKWELL**
born in Tarrytown, New York 8; death of his father 8-9; difficult child 12; decides to become an artist 12; indoctrinated into socialism 14; artistic vocation fostered by experience on Monhegan 18; falls in love with and marries Kathleen Whiting 23-4; renounces the "Better Self" in favor of the "Self" 25-6; first visit to Newfoundland 29-30; works in Minnesota 31-2; discovers a symbolic way of painting during second stay in Newfoundland 35-40; expelled from Newfoundland 36; moves to Staten Island 43; becomes "Hogarth, Jr." 46; affair with Hildegard Hirsch 46-8; travels to Alaska 51-5; spiritual transformation in Alaska 55-67; incorporates himself 69, 71; purchases "Egypt," a farm in Vermont 70, 72; affair with Lydia 76; travels to Tierra del Fuego 76-80; travels to Europe 79-80; distraught about missing Rocky at Brooklyn Docks 80; he and Kathleen agree to divorce 81; affair with Ernesta Drinker 81-2; marries Frances Lee Higgins 82-3; builds Asgaard 83-4; prolific book illustrator 85-92; travels in Greenland 93-6; social activism increases 97-100; moves to Asgaard 82-4; devotes a great of time to book illustration 85-92; several stays in Greenland 93-6; involvement with communism and socialist causes 97-9; problems running Asgaard 97-9; divorces Frances and marries Sally Johnston 100-1; involvement in cold war politics 103-6; market for his work declines 106; ill health and death 108-9

**BOOK ILLUSTRATIONS:**
*Beowulf* 86; Boccaccio *The Decameron* 86; Samuel Butler *Erewhon* 86; Chaucer, *Canterbury Tales* 85-6; Goethe, *Faust* 86; *The Jewel: A Romance of Fairyland* 47; Herman Melville, *Moby Dick* 2, 86-7, **88-9**, 92, 103; Njal saga 93; Pushkin, *The Gabrieliad* 85; *Saga of Gisli, Son of Sour* 86; Shakespeare *Plays* 86, *Venus and Adonis*, 86; Esther Shephard *Paul Bunyan* 86, **91**; Frederick Squires *Architec-tonics* 44, 85; Voltaire, *Candide* 2, 85; Walt Whitman 3, 13-4, 24; *Leaves of Grass* 71, 86-7, **90**, 92; Wilder, Thornton, *The Bridge of San Luis Rey* 2, 85

INDEX

**BOOKS**:
*It's Me O Lord* 4-5, 95, 107; *N by E* 94; *Salamina* 95; *This is My Own* 100, 107; *Voyaging: Southward from the Strait of Magellan* 78; *Wilderness: A Journal of Quiet Adventure in Alaska* 55, 70-1, 78, 87

**PAINTINGS**:
*Admiralty Sound, Tierra del Fuego* 78-**9**; *Alaska Winter* 53-**4**; *Asgaard Meadows* 108; *Autumn* 72; *Burial of a Young Man* 37-**8**; *December Eight, 1941 (The Open Road)* **102**; *Down to the Sea* **37**-8; *Early November, North Greenland* **96**; *Heavy, Heavy Hangs over Thy Head* [lithograph] **104**; *The House of Dread* **39**-40; *Men and Mountains* 26-**7**; *Newfoundland Dirge* 39; *North Wind* **55**; *Pastoral* 39; *Portrait of a Child (My Daughter Clara)* 40-**1**, 104; *Resurrection Bay – Alaska (Blue and Gold)* 53-**4**; *Shadows of Evening* 72' *Toilers of the Sea* 19-**20**; *The Trapper* 72-3; *Winter, Monhegan Island* 20-**1**; *A Young Sailor* 39

**SATIRICAL DRAWINGS**:
*The Bricklayer* 44; *New York Tribune* 75; "Plutarch's Lights of History," *Harper's Weekly*, 44; *Vanity Fair*, *Puck*, *A Basket of Poses*, and *Judge* 45-7

**SELF-PORTRAITS**:
*Portrait of Me Improved* **111**, 119; *Sea and Sky* **113**, 119; *Self-Portrait* **115**, 119; *Self-portrait, Voyaging* **117**, 119

**WILDERNESS**:
Dedication Page, **59**; Frontispiece **57**; *Home Building*, 56, **61**; *The Mad Hermit*, 56, **65**, 66; *On the Height*, 56, **63**; *Rain Torments*, 56; *Superman* 56; *Wilderness* 56

Kent, Rockwell III (Rocky), RK's son 24-5, 47-9, 51-2, 55-6, 80, 95
Kent, Sally Johnston, RK's third wife 100-2, 105, 109
Kent, Sara Holgate RK's mother 7-8, 11-2, 14, 19, 24-5, 32, 105, 107
Kent vs. Dulles 108
Kimmel, Michael 19
Kittredge, William, Lakeside Press 86
Klopfer, Donald 85
M. Knoedler & Co. 48, 70
Knopf, Alfred A. 2, 86
*Know and Defend* 102

Lakeside Press 86, 103
Lenin Peace Prize 108
Lobster Cove, Monhegan 19
Lord, Hewlett and Taylor 31
Lydia, the witch 76

Macbeth, William 30
Maine 4, 17-21, 23, 29, 66, 105-6
Manhasset, New York 72
Manigault, Edward Middleton 43-4
Manners, Marya 82
Marc, Franz 39
McCarthy, Joseph 106
Maureen 79
Melville, Herman, *Moby Dick* 2, 86-7, **88-9**, 92, 103
Metropolitan Museum of Art 48
Mielziner, Jo 97
Miller, Kenneth Hayes 13, 31
Miss Bennett's School for Girls 11
*The Modern School* 52
Monhegan, Maine 17-21, 23, 29, 66, 105-6
Monhegan Summer School 24

132

## INDEX

Moore, Raymond 97
Morris, Sir Edward 29-30
Munch, Edvard 39
Museum of Natural History, New York 86

*The Nation* 78
National Committee for Peoples' Rights 100
National Council of American-Soviet Friendship 108
New Bedford Whaling Museum 86
The New Deal 98, 103
Newfoundland 4, 29-30, 33, 35-40, 52, 93, 108
New Hampshire School of Art, Richmond 31
New London, Connecticut 43, 80
*New Republic* 78
*New Statesman* 71
New York City (Manhattan) 4, 8, 14, 24, 32, 66, 69
New York School of Art 12-3, 20, 24
New York State 4
Nietzche, Friedrich 4, 52-3, 70
Njal saga 93
North Sydney, Nova Scotia 29

Odysseus 75
Olson, Lars 52, 55, 76

*Painting and Drawings by Contemporary American Artists*, Old Harmonie Club 23
Pearmain, Nancy 31
Pearmain, Robert 31-2
Pène Du Bois, Guy 19
Peterborough, New Hampshire 46

Pittsfield, Massachusetts 25
Plattsburgh, New York 97, 109
"Plutarch's Lights of History," *Harper's Weekly* 44
Port aux Basques, Newfoundland 29
R. Prescott and Sons, Keeseville, New York 83
Proctor Marble Company, Barre Vermont 98
Progressive Party 103
*Puck* 45-6
Puerto Rico 98
Pulitzer, Ralph 72
Punta Arenas, Chile 77
Pushkin, Alexander *The Gabrieliad* 85
Putnam, George 70-1, 76
G.P. Putnam's Sons 70
Puvis de Chavannes 38

Random House 85
Rasmussen, Knud 94; *Across Arctic America* 94
Rio de Janeiro 100
Rockefeller, John D. 44
Romanoff, Michael Dimitri 99
Roosevelt, Franklin Delano 98, 103
Roosevelt, Theodore 19
Rosa, Austrian-born maid 8
Runge, Philipp Otto 40
Ryan, Joseph James 107
Ryan, Thomas Fortune 107
Ryder, Albert Pinkham 38

Sabin, Arthur J. 105
Sacco, Nicola and Bartolomeo Vanzetti 97
*Saga of Gisli, Son of Sour* 86

INDEX

St. John's, Newfoundland 35-6
Salamina 95
Seward, Alaska 51
Shakespeare the *Plays, Venus and Adonis* 2, 86
*Shanghai* 80
Shephard, Esther *Paul Bunyan* 86, **91**
Shinnecock, Baytown, Long Island, New York 8, 12
Shinnecock Hills Summer School 12
Sloan, John 13
Smallwood, Joey 108
Society of American Artists 17
Southern Pacific Railway 48
Soviet Academy of Fine Arts 108
Squires, Frederick *Architec-tonics* 44, 85
*S.S. Homeric* 80
*S.S. Newfoundland* 35
*S.S. Southern Cross* 35
Staten Island, New York 43
Sterling, Jane Bell (Jennie) 24-5, 29-30, 46-7
Sterner, Marie 48, 69-71
Stockholm Appeal and the World Peace Council 105
Strait of Magellan, Chile 77
Strindberg, August 39
Symbolism 39-40

Tarrytown New York 4, 8
Thayer, Abbott Handerson 13-4, 18, 23, 25
Thayer, Gerald 23, 25
Thoreau, Henry David 3, 13-4, 24
Thwaites, John E. 51
Tierra del Fuego 4, 75-8
Tolstoy, Leo 53

Un-American Activities committee 104
Union League 30
Untermeyer, Louis 95
Ushuaia, Beagle Channel, Tierra del Fuego 77
USSR 101, 108

Vanderbilt, Frederika 72
*Vanity Fair* 44-**5**, 46, 87
Vargas, Getúlio 100
Vermont 75-6
Voltaire, *Candide* 2, 85

Wallace, Henry 103-4
Watrous, Harry 30
Watson, Forbes, *The Evening Post* 21
Weeks, Rufus 14
Wells, F. DeWitt 79-80
Weyhe Gallery 83
Whitman, Walt 3, 13-4, 24; *Leaves of Grass* 71, 86-7, **90**, 92
Whitneys 72
Wien, Jake Milgram 38, 44, 100
Wildenstein Galleries 83
Wilder, Thornton, *The Bridge of San Luis Rey* 2, 85
Winona, Minnesota 31
Woodstock, New York 83
World War I 36, 43
World War II 101-2

Ytterock, Ole 77

Ziegfield Follies 46
Zigrosser, Carl 52, 67, 69, 72, 76-7, 86

# Dissident Biographies

Series Editor: Dr Rohan Price, University of Tasmania

Who do you know who changed the way that we think about the world?

*Dissident Biographies* is a landmark new series open to short biographical accounts of contrarian individuals who lived according to the edicts of their heart to make an impact in history. The series calls on authors to critically explore interactions between ideas and experience through the medium of biography. Its aim is to show the determinist impact of intellectual ideas on lives, movements and the sweep of history. Some of these biographies will polarise; others will reconcile or legitimate in retrospect.

The editors seek to enable perspectives of equity, diversity and inclusion. We celebrate life accounts driven by the experience of marginalized communities emphasising the underrepresented within public discourse. The series is open to scholars and public intellectuals working in all areas of the humanities and social sciences, avowing an interdisciplinary or even post-disciplinary approach.

Within a limit of 40, 000 words you are expected to identify key moments in the awakening of a new ideal. How and why did it arise in the subject's life? What was disruptive about its realisation? What attempts were made to silence it? How has this been noticed in history or activism? You will tease out how the subject's ideas impacted their time as a catalyst or provocation for contemporaries and, via memory, for future generations.

Authors are charged to produce an exciting, provocative and even polemical account of a life that is misunderstood, underrated or influential.

For more information, please contact Series Editor Dr Rohan Price (rohan.price@utas.edu.au) or Senior Acquisitions Editor Dr Philip Dunshea (p.dunshea@peterlang.com).

www.ingramcontent.com/pod-product-compliance
Lightning Source LLC
Chambersburg PA
CBHW071209240526
45470CB00018B/1647